A BRIEF HISTORY OF
THE COLONIAL WARS
IN AMERICA
FROM 1607 TO 1775

COLONIAL SENTINEL GUARDING THE VILLAGE AT FORT BEDFORD

A BRIEF HISTORY OF THE COLONIAL WARS IN AMERICA FROM 1607 TO 1775

FOR THE ENLIGHTENMENT OF THE PRESENT GENERATION ABOUT THE ACTIVITIES OF THE EARLY AMERICAN PATRIOTS BEFORE THE REVOLUTION

HERBERT TREADWELL WADE

COACHWHIP PUBLICATIONS
Greenville, Ohio

A Brief History of the Colonial Wars in America . . .,
    by Herbert Treadwell Wade
© 2022 Coachwhip Publications edition

First published 1948 by The Society of Colonial Wars
Herbert Treadwell Wade, 1872-1955
CoachwhipBooks.com

ISBN 1-61646-539-5
ISBN-13 978-1-61646-539-1

TABLE OF CONTENTS

CHRONOLOGY OF COLONIAL PERIOD

1607, MAY 3	Jamestown, Virginia, founded.
1609, SEPT. 3	Henry Hudson enters New York Bay.
1614	Atlantic coast explored and mapped by Captain John Smith.
1620, DEC. 11-21	Pilgrims arrive at Plymouth, Massachusetts.
1626	New Amsterdam founded. Manhattan Island purchased from Indians.
1628	Acadia and Quebec captured by English.
1634, MARCH	Maryland founded.
1637, MAY 1	Connecticut General Court declares war on Pequot Indians.
1643, MAY 19	New England Federation formed.
1651-1673	English Navigation Laws.
1652	New Amsterdam incorporated as a city.
1659-1697	King William's War.
1663	Grant of Carolina to eight Lord Proprietors.
1664	English take New Amsterdam.
1675-1676	King Philip's War in New England.
1675, DEC. 19	Great Swamp Fight.
1676	Bacon's Rebellion in Virginia.
1686	Dominion of New England formed by consolidation of colonies.

1690, MAY 11	English capture Port Royal.
1702-1713	Queen Anne's War (War of the Spanish Succession).
1702	St. Augustine captured and burned by English.
1704, FEB. 29	Deerfield Massacre.
1710	Acadia attacked and Port Royal Captured by New England Colonists.
1711	Tuscarora War in North Carolina.
1715	Defeat of Yamassees and other Indian tribes in North Carolina.
1733	Georgia founded.
1739-1745	War between Spain and England.
1743-1748	King George's War.
1745, JUNE	Capture of Louisbourg by Sir William Pepperrell and New England troops.
1753	French occupy Ohio country.
1754	Fort Necessity captured by French.
1755-1763	French and Indian War (Seven Years War).
1755, JULY 9	British under Braddock defeated at Fort Du Quesne.
1755, SEPT. 8	Battle of Lake George. French defeated.
1756, MAY	England declares war on France.
1756, AUG. 14	Montcalm captures Forts Oswego and George.
1757, AUG. 9	Montcalm takes Fort William Henry.
1758, JULY 8	British defeated at Ticonderoga.
1758, JULY 26	Second capture of Louisbourg by Gen. Jeffrey Amherst.
1758, AUG. 27	Fort Frontenac, captured by Col. John Bradstreet.
1758, NOV. 25	Capture of Fort Du Quesne by Gen. John Forbes.
1759, JULY 25	Fort Niagara captured and French driven from Western New York.

1759, Aug.	Ticonderoga abandoned by French.
1759, Sept. 13	Battle of Plains of Abraham, Quebec. Death of Montcalm and Wolfe.
1763, Feb. 10	Treaty of Paris ending French and Indian War.

From the Painting by H. A. Ogden. (c) Yale University Press

AMERICAN AND BRITISH UNIFORMS, FRENCH AND INDIAN WARS,
1754-1763

From. Vol. 6, "The Pageant of America"

FOREWORD

In 1947, the Society of Colonial Wars in the State of New York printed and circulated several thousand lists of preferred reading on the American Colonial Period. They were sent to libraries, schools, patriotic societies, newspapers, magazines and, to a limited extent, to the general public in the thirteen original states.

In an endeavor to stimulate the study of early American Colonial history, this list included works of historical importance, original narratives, fiction, and references to the social background of provincial life. It is here reprinted as a bibliography.

The interest shown by those who received this bibliography has prompted the Society to republish, in pamphlet form, the summaries of the various Colonial Wars, which appeared in its Fiftieth Anniversary monograph, so that they might have a wider distribution.

Members of various groups which are interested in special periods of American history are concerned more with the events that led to our freedom than in the participation of their forebears. Instead of magnifying individual achievements and assuming reflected credit, members of these societies believe that by emulating the courage, fortitude and independence of the early pioneers of our country, they can contribute to the betterment of American life and be more worthy of their heritage. Particularly in connection with the various political and military operations of the seventeenth and early eighteenth centuries, it should be recalled that the important results of the French and Indian wars were to establish in North America the political and cultural dominance of Anglo-Saxon rather than French ideas and ideologies leading to democratic government and the freedom of the individual. With this broad purpose, these brief accounts of American Colonial martial achievements are made available to schools, libraries and the public.

MESSMORE KENDALL
Governor of the Society

Publication Committee
LESTER DURAND GARDNER
GEORGE FREDERICK MILES
HERBERT TREADWELL WADE

THE COLONIAL WARS IN AMERICA

The period in American history which the Society of Colonial Wars seeks to commemorate is replete with striking and significant events which merit an importance for later generations far beyond their powers to realize and appreciate. This American Colonial period stands unique in history for its evolution of new and fundamental ideas in social, political, and religious fields. The pioneer settlements developed a culture which, stemming from old-world ideas, produced a civilization on which was founded the America of today.

There were involved in these Colonial days not only men of enterprise, bravery, and a pioneering spirit, but strong men with a devotion to principle and a readiness to risk life and property in founding communities where, under conditions of personal and political liberty and opportunity, they could live. Here they dwelt not only in happiness and prosperity, but in the hope of a new world, where every man had his chance for advancement along with a mode of life vastly superior to that he had known in Europe.

INCENTIVES AND OBJECTIVES

In New England in particular, in addition to the opportunities for economic and industrial independence open to the individual, there was the further and important consideration that for the first time the family and family life was playing an important part in the general scheme of colonization and settlement. Accordingly, to the safeguarding of the occupied land and the attendant economic enterprises there was added the incentive of adequate protection of wife, children, and home, either as a part of a small community or as a constituent element of a larger political unit.

The presence of the family established a different basis of life and a desire for a fuller communal existence than was to be realized at the trading post or fishing station elsewhere in the world, and this in turn made proper and adequate defence an early and immediate essential. A home with farm or garden was indeed a different matter from a garrison, and its protection along with neighboring homes and settlements early became the first consideration common to all the colonies.

Of course self-preservation was the first task of the colonist and he and his family at once had to accustom themselves to the rigors of a harsh and unfriendly climate, and the inevitable privations and deficiencies in housing and subsistence involved in an early pioneering existence. With these early conditions overcome, local protection against wild animals and Indians came to the fore with some form of organized and controlled effort.

The first step was the night watch maintained by the constables and centering at the meeting-house, in which each citizen was required to take part. This also involved the carrying of arms to church services and other assemblies, and the maintenance of adequate supplies of weapons and ammunition. As the towns and villages increased in population such defence might seem adequate, but at no great distance there might be serious threats of marauding

DANGER FROM THE INDIANS OF OUR FOREFATHERS

tribes on the warpath. Then further and more formal organization was found in train-bands with permanent officers and regular drill or exercise. Naturally this led to a county or regimental organization with appropriate officers, and practically universal service was required of all able-bodied male citizens within certain age limits.

INDIAN ATTACKS—NORTH AND SOUTH

For such general and threatening activities as came in the Pequot War and King Philip's War and Indian attacks in the Southern colonies, the central government would call out colonial forces to act as a unit under commanding officers selected by the councils of the individual colonies.

As distinct from New England the population of the Southern colonies was much less dense, and agriculture involving large plantations became more extended than commerce and industry which were slower to develop. However, quite early all the colonies made progress in a commerce based on the interchange of products by sea not only among themselves but with Europe and the West Indies. Naturally the first menace was the Indian, the hazard of course varying in different places and times, but for a number of years it rather increased than diminished, taking the colonies as a whole.

Later and too often in connection with the Indians, came the consideration of defence against enemies and causes which for the settler seemed far removed from his daily and immediate concerns. In other words soon there was to be brought to the very doors of the colonists European conflicts which involved Indian alliances as well as the presence of European soldiery and battles fought where European warfare was combined with the savage arts of the aborigine.

From the Painting by H. A. Ogden.   (c) Yale University Press

FRENCH UNIFORMS, FRENCH AND INDIAN WARS, 1754-1763

From. Vol. 6, "The Pageant of America"

Safety First Aim of the Colonists

To the average man in the American Colonies politics and religious disputations were far removed except as they enabled him to lead a fuller and more comfortable life, but they have bulked large in contemporary history. In fact quite a few historians assert that the emigrants who left European homes for religious reasons usually exhibited not only greater independence but greater intelligence and vigor of action than those who remained at home. But in all the colonies there was in progress the evolution of a suitable government and a system of administration which held the attention of the leaders both lay and ecclesiastic. In the background there was the inescapable fact that the safety of individuals and communities must be maintained. Later came the larger question of the safety of the colony itself and its neighbors, requiring some cooperative action. And it may be emphasized that in each of the colonies defence, military organization, and participation in greater or less hostilities over a period of more than 150 years certainly had their effect on moulding the characters of our ancestors and the nation they founded.

In the present review it is desirable to consider the question of defence and military activity as it concerned the colonists, realizing of course that while absolutely essential from their earliest days it was by no means the predominant consideration or influence in the evolution of these provincial states and resulting civilization. In fact the colonist first of all was most concerned with his daily struggle for existence and his private affairs as involved in the clearance and tillage of the land, the construction of his dwelling house, and such commercial ventures as were concerned with the fisheries, fur trade, lumbering, and the supply and distribution of the various necessities required by the settlers in his own or other colonies. Thus there was developed a commerce and often local industries on a small scale that made for ever-increasing wealth and a higher standard of living.

In the Southern colonies conditions in a way were somewhat different due largely to their various charters and economic and geographical conditions under which they operated. With proprietors or chartered companies functioning under Royal grants there was less opportunity for democratic activity and individual advancement as found in the Northern colonies. Such feeling was far from absent and Bacon's Rebellion in Virginia and other manifestations indicated that here also the spirit of freedom found expression in various ways at times of political differences with governors, proprietors, councils, and assemblies.

COLONIES ALONG THE ATLANTIC COAST

Here it may be emphasized that from New England to Georgia the colonists occupied a strip along the Atlantic coast, but as they pushed their frontiers inland with the increase of new immigration there inevitably resulted hostilities, with the Indians forced out of their lands and the possibility of conflict with the French and, in the South, with the Spanish.

Thus the Colonial Wars must be considered in a broader relation than in an independent or local aspect, for it will appear that Colonial military forces were closely connected with external as well as internal circumstances as the provinces grew in wealth and numbers. While differences of opinion might develop between the Colonies and the Crown over chartered rights and other political and administrative matters, yet when world-wide hostilities developed it was recognized that Royal troops and navy must enter into the consideration and that harmony of action was essential.

The colonies on the eastern Atlantic coast in the main were settled by the English or under English auspices

From the Painting by C. W. Jefferys. (c) Yale University Press

FIRST INLAND MEETING OF THE FRENCH AND BRITISH, 1666

From. Vol. 8, "The Pageant of America"

where there was no intrinsic racial hatred of the English and their institutions, save when monarchial or ecclesiastical tyranny was exerted or legitimate political differences developed. The Dutch who settled in New Amsterdam did not continue in possession of that province after 1664, when it was yielded to the English, while the Swedes, colonizing along the Delaware River after 1638, were but lukewarm in their loyalties to the home land or at least lacked the numbers and strength to resist the aggression of the Dutch to whom they yielded in 1655.

Accordingly, the prevalence of such feelings on the part of the colonists meant that when England came to be involved in such wars as developed with France or Spain their sympathies naturally followed England, to the extent of organizing expeditions against the enemy colonies or islands. Later it was impossible for them to assume an attitude of isolation, even were it desired, notwithstanding their aloofness from the original causes of many of the controversies.

American Colonies Involved in European Wars

This naturally led to the phase of the matter, where English colonies in the New World at once became not only vulnerable targets of attack, but also afforded convenient bases from which the forces of the British Empire might strike at the enemy. Such conditions inevitably served to involve the colonists in numerous military activities from 1607 to 1775, and participation in what might be termed world wars involved serious casualties and outlay of treasure by relatively young and struggling provinces which could ill afford such drafts on their population or wealth.

Then there was the further consideration of Indian attacks, already mentioned, which from being at first a local matter soon involved reprisals and developed into prolonged conflicts. For these often the colonists were far from blameless, but in one form or another they took a serious toll of life and resources, and were attended by savageries and barbarities with a brutalizing effect on the settler. A natural consequence of these savage uprisings was that the eastern Indians soon aligned themselves with one or the other of the European powers contending for the mastery of the New World.

Obviously this involved serious measures of organized defence related to and a part of the provincial government, which, developing from the night watches of the first settlements to the organized forces that later fought with Amherst and Wolfe against Montcalm and the French, represented a growing consciousness of necessary protection for the new towns and villages at ever increasing distances from the seacoast and the larger centres of population.

The achievement of religious freedom, the political evolution of a self-governing state, and the development of economic independence and industrial prosperity, usually are given far greater stress than matters of defence in considering colonial history, but the martial tradition of the colonial soldier and his training produced the men who fought to success the American Revolution.

AMERICAN COLONIES INVOLVED IN EUROPEAN WARS

Following as it did democratic lines, there unavoidably resulted at times inefficiency and lack of responsibility which too often marked the colonial militia, but there was the patriotic fervor of the free citizen, and the feeling that he as an individual was part of a cause he could understand. Colonial and Revolutionary America was not solely the achievement of the soldier, but his service certainly started the American tradition of loyalty, devotion and sacrifice, which, whenever called upon in times of need,

ELLIOT INSTRUCTING THE INDIANS

never have been lacking to support with arms and life the principles of liberty and democracy when assailed by a foreign foe.

Such military activities in colonial days naturally may be grouped in certain conflicts to which definite names are given, but it must be realized that the evolution of defence, formal and otherwise, followed the political and economic progress as population grew and improved standards of life and civic development followed. But such activity was in no way restricted to these main conflicts, for with the Indians for many years as a perpetual menace and border outbreaks to be guarded against, the colonist was rarely free from the threat of attack from an enemy at his outposts.

Thus aside from Indian or purely local conflicts during the seventeenth and eighteenth centuries, there were four major wars fought in part on the North American continent and vitally concerning the English colonists, though they themselves for the most part were not directly responsible for these conflicts.

In 1689 came King William's War, followed in 1702 by Queen Anne's War which lasted until 1713. Then came King George's War in 1744-1745, and finally came the Seven Years War or the French and Indian War lasting from 1756 to 1763. As these wars between France and England are viewed from the distance of time it is quite apparent that there was involved not only a struggle for a vast territory continually increasing in strategic and economic importance, but also a contest of two radically different systems of imperial power and government.

French and Spanish Threats

From the earliest days of the English colonies the French in Canada were a threat to New England and to New York while South Carolina and later Georgia became an English frontier against the Spaniards in Florida and the

French and Spaniards in the West Indies. As a result, in
Georgia compulsory military drill was enforced early. In
other words in the two Carolinas and in Georgia English
and Spanish long were in conflict and foreign invasion
often was as present a danger as Indian attacks. Thus the
Governor and Council at Charleston in 1708 reported to
the Lords Proprietors in London, "St. Augustine, a Spanish garrison being planted to the southward of us about a
hundred leagues makes Carolina a frontier to all the English Settlements on the main."

The last of the wars above mentioned accordingly resolved itself into a contest definite and final, fought to
determine whether England or France should dominate the
North American continent, and naturally brought home to
the colonists the vital question of the survival of a civilization they had developed, with the attendant ideas of
political and religious liberty and opportunity for individual advancement.

In these struggles, war which they might have thought
to avoid in the migration from Europe, was brought home
to the American colonist, but it was clear to him that he
did not go out seeking conquest and territorial aggrandize-
ment but merely the preservation of what he had achieved
and for what he was ready to lay down his life.

But for England and France went the important stake
of the unconquered and unsettled West, to which no definite title could be claimed save that won by exploration
and settlement, and which by whomsoever occupied naturally was a threat to outlying regions of the more venture-
some pioneers.

Intercolonial trade as between Boston and the Carolinas did much to bring the American colonies together
and the passage of various Navigation Acts unfavorably
affected colonial trade and shipping. The second Navigation Act, 1663, forbade the carrying of produce of English

plantations anywhere except to other plantations until it had been first landed in England. In resistance to such measures there was early found a bond of union between the American colonies.

The colonial militia which, organized and extended as the needs arose, as in the various wars, was a democratic development with officers chosen by the citizens themselves or by their elected representatives. Here the aim was so to distribute service that an individual might share equitably with his fellows the requirements of duty. As the calls for colonial troops for service at some distance from the home community came, or as the gravity of invasion or attack increased and the menaces of war brought by a foreign foe or the need of co-operation with the forces from England, there was presented to the colonies at times the problem of uniting the constituent elements of military strength when the colonies themselves had but the slightest bonds in a common loyalty.

While the various colonies had marked differences of culture and political life, it developed that many of their problems were very similar and these included not only questions of defence, but also political independence, or perhaps interdependence and commerce. While settlers in the different colonies varied considerably in wealth and opportunities due to conditions of geography and national origins, yet to a surprising degree there were common interests either latent or in course of development.

In this connection it should be remembered that the colonies North and South both were affected and when the French and Spanish attacked either on land or sea there resulted not only a harmony of interest but a tendency towards co-operation, that by the time of the French and Indian wars implied the germs of a nascent nationalism.

The Elizabethan world struggle between England and Spain had its climax and eclipse on the coast of the

THE LAKE GEORGE BATTLE MONUMENT OF THE SOCIETY
OF COLONIAL WARS

Carolinas and Georgia, bringing as it did piracy and buc-caneering to the Atlantic shores of North America in a more or less intimate way, and Spain became a potential and at times active enemy of the Southern colonies during the seventeenth and eighteenth centuries.

It can hardly be said the growth in organization for defence in the American Colonies corresponded with their economic and political development, and democrat-ic methods inevitably brought results of varying military efficiency. But such service had its effect on the progress of American ideals and American culture and civilization. In other words, there may be seen in the military orga-nization and development of the American colonies that distinct individualism and democracy which had not only immediate effects but a profound and lasting influence on the Colonies as a whole as regards their martial effort and which continued later after the establishment of the American Republic.

LOYALTY TO THE ENGLISH CROWN

This included not only a patriotic fervor and sense of re-sponsibility as well as loyalty to the Crown, but also there was developed individual initiative and adaptability to the military problems in hand, particularly as influenced and conditioned by special local conditions of terrain. Such characteristics, as produced in the country fought over and against the native Indian foe, served not only in the expe-ditions and objectives of the day but became pre-eminent in the French and Indian War and later in the American Revolution, not to mention subsequent conflicts waged in North America.

But it must not be understood that the military achievements of our colonial ancestors always were above criticism, or that the work of individuals or of the colo-nial forces operating as greater or smaller units was always successful or blameless. In fact the best of our modern historians of this period have brought to light many such deficiencies, not in a spirit of captious fault-finding or sensational deflation of men and measures, but as parts of a larger picture which it is desired to study in its completeness, not only as contributing the necessary contrast in such a study but as indicating the evolutionary development of the future American Army.

Taking as an instance the soldiers of the French and Indian War who became important commanders in the Army of the American Revolution, many had had the experience of actual field and combat service in the earlier struggle. On such a roll would be found the names of George Washington, Israel Putnam, John Stark, Philip Schuyler, Charles Lee, Horatio Gates, Daniel Morgan, John Armstrong, William Mercer, Artemas Ward, Richard Montgomery, William Prescott, and Richard Gridley.

LEADERS FOR THE AMERICAN REVOLUTION EMERGE

The Continental Congress at its meeting held on June 17, 1775, elected Artemas Ward and Charles Lee major-generals to serve with Washington, who had been made commander-in-chief on June 15th of that year. On June 9th, Philip Schuyler was chosen third major-general, and Israel Putnam fourth. On June 22, 1775, of the eight brigadier-generals chosen, Pomeroy, Montgomery, Wooster, Heath, Spencer, and Thomas, and the adjutant-general Horatio Gates, had served in the French and Indian War.

INTERIOR OF AN INDIAN VILLAGE

From Vol. 2, "History of the American People" by Woodrow Wilson

INDIAN WARS IN NEW ENGLAND

From the time of the Settlement at Plymouth in 1620 and the advent of the Massachusetts Bay Colony in 1630 there had been bitter disputes and conflicts with the Indians, though at times and places there were more amicable relations. Such untoward incidents, irrespective of the causes directly responsible for them, too seldom were marked by constant and pronounced highmindedness on the part of the settlers. It was the beginning of a conflict of races and civilizations, a condition that from the beginnings of history had led to the inevitable result the world over, that one or the other must be eliminated if not in warfare at least by economic pressure. And this, too, is usually irrespective of the abstract ethics involved or the conduct of the parties.

As the individual incidents at this time involving the killing of both settlers and Indians became more frequent, a crisis was reached on May 1, 1637, when the Connecticut General Court declared war on the Pequots, a Mohegan tribe living on the Connecticut shore from the Rhode Island boundary west to the Thames and Connecticut rivers. This colony sought the cooperation of both Plymouth and Massachusetts Bay in the development of a punitive or avenging expedition. This may be considered the first Indian war of the Colonies, and it was the beginning of what soon became either forcible expulsion of the Indians from the English settlements, or the eventual annihilation of such as sought to remain and contest the ground. But this was a prolonged process and involved attacks and massacres and reprisals by the Colonists.

As is the case with many of the important events in the Colonial Wars the Pequot War was the subject of an interesting paper presented before the Society by Robert Dewey Benedict, a member, on December 19, 1899, and printed in the 1906-1907 Year Book. Some significant extracts from this paper are presented herewith and afford a summary of the Pequot War.

THE PEQUOT WAR

"The number of the combatants in that war were very unequal. The English settlements of Connecticut were on the Connecticut River in the towns of Hartford, Windsor and Wethersfield, whither a company of settlers had come from Massachusetts Bay through the woods only the year before. In 1637 there were probably 160 or 170 families, making about 800 persons. There was also a garrison of 20 men in the fort at the mouth of the river. The Pequots occupied that part of Connecticut east of the Connecticut River. East of them to Narragansett Bay were the Narragansetts, whose chief was Miantonomo, and north of them were the Mohegans, under the leadership of Uncas. . .

"In 1634 a Captain Stone, bound from Plymouth to Virginia in a pinnace, stopped in the Connecticut River, and was there set upon by the Pequots, and he and his men were all killed, and the vessel taken. Not long after this the Pequots sent messengers and gifts to the Massachusetts Colony, desiring friendship. An agreement was made by which those Indians who were guilty of Stone's death were to be given up to the English, although the Pequot messengers defended themselves as to that, claiming that Stone had been killed in a just quarrel."

THE UNRELIABLE PEQUOTS

It was also agreed that the English might settle in Connecticut if they wished, and that the English should mediate a peace between the Pequots and the Narragansetts. But the Pequots failed to comply with their agreements, and the next year, one John Oldham, trading in a small vessel at Block Island, was killed with his men, and his vessel plundered by the Indians there, who were under Pequot control, and were afterwards sheltered by the Pequots. Thereupon the Bay Colony sent an expedition of one hundred men under command of Captain Endicott, to obtain satisfaction. Endicott demanded the heads of the men who had killed Stone and his company, whom in the treaty the Pequots had agreed to give up. An ambassador from the Pequots temporized, asked for time to confer with the sachems, and then reported that the sachems were not at home, but were gone to Long Island. Thereupon the English, seeing that they were thus put off and that the Pequots were preparing to disappear in the wilderness, would wait no longer, but landed on both sides of the river, burned wigwams, and spoiled the corn.

"This expedition must be considered the beginning of the Pequot War. As is not uncommon, each side charged the other party with being the aggressor. The Connecticut colonists urged the leaders of the other colonies to join them in an attack upon the Pequots, in early spring, and Massachusetts Bay had agreed, but Plymouth had not agreed—did not agree till June, when help was no longer needed. And before any help at all had arrived an attack by the Pequots on Wethersfield, in which nine of the English were killed, and two young women were carried away captive, forced it upon the Connecticut men whether it were wiser for them to wait still longer, leaving the Pequots free to waylay them as they should choose, or to protect

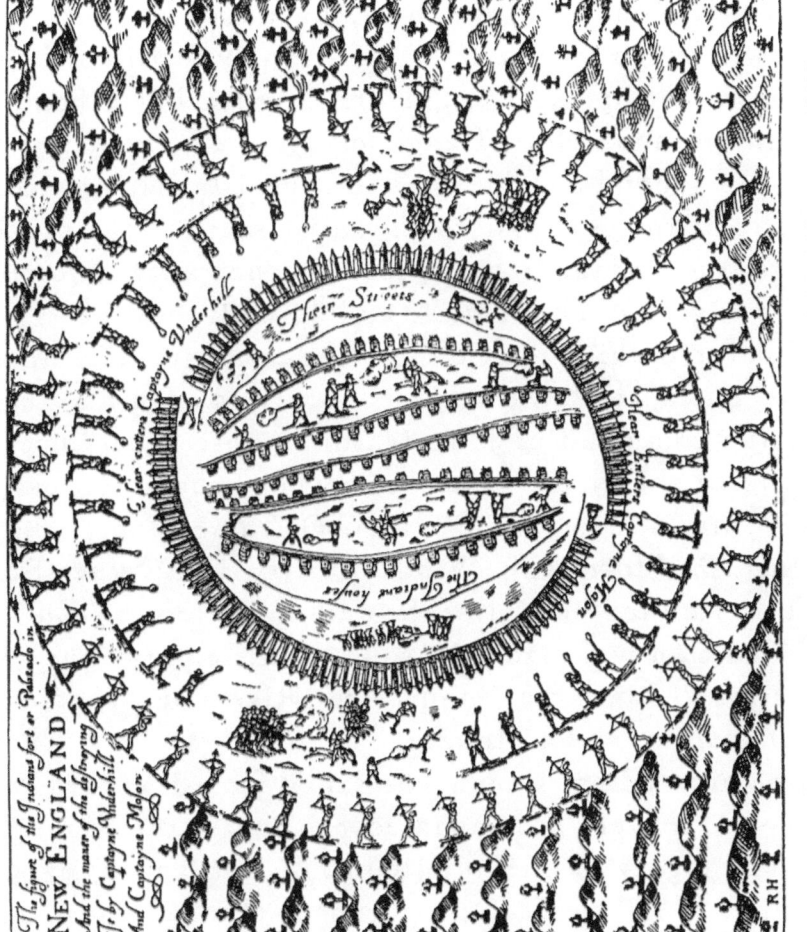

THE PEQUOT FORT CAPTURED BY CAPTAINS UNDERHILL AND MASON.
MAY 26, 1637

their homes by carrying the war into the territory of their enemies."

Pequots Strongly Fortified

"On May 1, 1637, a General Court of the three Connecticut towns was held at Hartford, at which they 'seriously considered their condition, which did look very sad, for those Pequots were a great people, being strongly fortified, cruel, warlike, munitioned, etc., and the English but a handful in comparison. It pleased God so to stir up the hearts of all men in general and the Court in special, that they concluded some forces should forthwith be sent out against the Pequots, their grounds being just and necessity enforcing them to engage in an offensive and defensive war.'

"The force which the Connecticut colonists determined to send out against the Pequots consisted of ninety men under the command of John Mason, whose experience in the wars of the Netherlands, and whose character, easily pointed him out to be the leader. Of these ninety, Hartford furnished forty-two, Windsor thirty, and Wethersfield eighteen. And ten days after the determination to send out the expedition was made, Mason and his eighty-nine soldiers started down the Connecticut River, on board of a pink, a shallop, and a pinnace. . .

"The ninety Englishmen who sailed from Hartford that tenth of May were accompanied by Uncas, the Mohegan chief, and eighty or one hundred of his Indians. They had fifty miles to sail to reach the fort at Saybrook, where they were to determine on the plan of campaign. . .

"The fort was commanded by Captain Lion Gardiner, who became the owner of Gardiner's Island, and from whom it received its name. With him was Captain John Underhill, who had been sent forward with twenty men from Massachusetts to strengthen the garrison. . .

Observing the Sabbath

"The expedition went up Narragansett Bay, Bancroft tells us, as far as Wickford. I do not know on what authority this statement is made. It is probable that if they did go up so far, it was because they wished to be as near as possible to the dwelling-place of Canonicus, one of the Narragansett Chiefs, with whom they wished to confer. They reached their desired port, Mason says, on Saturday, towards afternoon. And 'there,' he adds, 'we kept the Sabbath.' . . .

"Mason had an interview with Miantonomo, the chief sachem of the Narragansetts, the result of which was that the chiefs not only allowed the English to pass through their lands to attack the Pequots, but gave permission to the Narragansetts to join the expedition, which several hundred of them did. . .

"The fort which they finally determined to assault was composed of palisades enclosing about an acre, or perhaps two, of ground. The palisades were driven into the ground some three or four feet, and were ten or twelve feet high, not standing quite close together. There were two entrances, one on the northeast, and the other on the southwest side, which were closed by a bar and some bushes. Within this palisade were about seventy wigwams. The number of the Indians occupying them is variously estimated at from 500 to 800.

"The Englishmen marched, accompanied by their Indian allies, some fifteen or twenty miles on the first day, to a fort of the Narragansetts, which the Narragansett Chief who held it refused to allow them to enter. About eight o'clock on Thursday morning the English took up their march again, the Indian contingent having risen by this time to about 500. They marched about twelve miles to a fjord of the Pawcatuck River where they halted. The day was very hot. Their provisions were very scanty, and some of their men had fainted from heat and toil.

"They marched on through the afternoon, and until the middle of the night. They must have crossed the Mystic River near its source, so that they came down from the northeast towards the Pequot fort which they had determined to assault. And when within about two miles of the fort, they pitched their little camp between two hillocks, which are now known as Porter's Rocks. Mason says, 'We were much wearied with hard Travel, keeping great Silence, supposing we were very near the Fort, as our Indians informed us, which proved otherwise; the Rocks were our Pillows; yet Rest was pleasant; the Night proved Comfortable, being clear and Moon Light. We appointed out Guards and placed our Sentinels at some distance, who heard the Enemy Singing at the Fort, who continued the Strain until Midnight, with great Insulting and Rejoycing, as we were afterwards informed.'"

THE ATTACK

The colonists made their attack early in the morning, intending to enter both entrances simultaneously. The Indians were surprised and after slight resistance the wigwams were fired and those that were not burned to death perished by shot and sword. In little more than an hour's space the fort considered impregnable by the Indians was utterly destroyed and some six or seven hundred perished. Only seven were taken captive and about seven escaped.

The colonists suffered a loss of two slain outright and about twenty were wounded. Their provisions and munitions were nearly spent so that they were glad to hear of the arrival of their vessels sailing into Pequot Harbor. However, before these could be reached the Indians from the other fort approached, and a second action occurred in which the attackers were again worsted. On the way to the ships more wigwams were fired and the Indians put to rout.

Captain Mason and his men marched to Saybrook and later their services were recognized by the General Court on November 14th, making appropriation for liberal payment to the common soldiers of the expedition.

"The spirit of the tribe was so broken that they thought of nothing but flight to some region where they could be safe from an enemy whose power they had found to be so terrible. They burned their other fort, their wigwams, and what stores they could not carry with them, and betook themselves to the wild woods west of the Connecticut. About a month after the Mystic fight, one hundred and twenty men of the Massachusetts force which had been raised for the war, under Captain Stoughton, reached the Saybrook fort, and it was then resolved to pursue the remains of the tribe, till its utter destruction should be a permanent warning to all the Indian tribes. Mason and forty Connecticut men were again on foot and the English men marched westward, finding here and there some scattering Pequots, and finally traced the main body of the fugitives into a swamp in the town of Fairfield. Their first attack was repulsed by the Pequots whereupon the English surrounded the swamp. The warriors in the swamp made a brave fight. Some 60 or 70 broke through the English lines in the morning fog and made their escape. The rest were killed or taken prisoners."

THE LAST OF THE PEQUOTS

The few remaining Pequots perished either at the hands of their Indian enemies or surrendered unconditionally to the whites, and the few survivors of a once powerful tribe were divided among the Mohegans and the Narragansetts, never more to be called the Pequots. The name Pequot was taken away from the river around which they lived in 1658, after which date it was called the Thames.

GOVERNOR BERKELEY DEFYING BACON'S DEMAND FOR A COMMISSION

VIRGINIA AND BACON'S REBELLION

In the Colony of Virginia the conflicts of the settlers with the Indians while more or less continuous hardly involved such organized expeditions as described in New England, but the Indian massacre of March 22, 1622 led to various political changes in the colony. The coming of Sir William Berkeley as Governor in 1642 resulted in distinct economic advances as well as measures against the hostile Indians. In 1644, the year of the second great massacre of the whites, he marched at the head of a small army and defeated the savages, obtaining a peace that lasted for more than a generation.

At the time of the war of the English with the Dutch in 1665, Virginia military forces were placed on a high plane of efficiency, and the merchant shipping of the Colony was armed to resist the attacks of the Dutch Navy which were stopped short of any invasion on land.

GOVERNOR BERKELEY'S ADMINISTRATION

It was during Berkeley's administration that the democratic uprising known as Bacon's Rebellion occurred in 1676 after an Indian invasion in the previous year. Nathaniel Bacon, a young man of twenty-eight, owner of two plantations on the James River near Richmond was made a member of the Governor's Council, a great honor for such a young man. Virginia was ripe for a leader who dared to oppose the growing abuses of Governor Berkeley's aging authority. The House of Burgesses had been kept in session continuously for fifteen years without any reelection, by the expedient of adjournments. The price of tobacco had been kept scandalously low by the oppressive English navigation laws which forbade trade by the planters with other countries than England. The King had given large grants of land to his favorites and sent others to be given lucrative positions in the colonial administration. But it was Berkeley's hesitation to join open conflict with the Indians that was the spark that set fire to the magazine of protest that was to lead to the earliest open rebellion in America against the King's representative in a colony.

In January 1696, thirty-six people were murdered by the Indians. Sixty plantations had been destroyed in seventeen days. Reports came to the Virginians of the havoc King Philip was making in New England and the vengeance wrought there by the terrified citizenry. Sir William Berkeley forbade the taking up of arms against the Indian enemies and asserted that the frontier forts afforded all the protection needed.

Bacon heard, early in May 1676, that a band of Indians had attacked his upper estate and killed his overseer and a servant. He assembled an armed group of planters and was chosen their leader. He sent a request to the Governor asking for a commission. Berkeley's reply was evasive but Bacon assumed command and started to march against the Indians. He had not gone far when he was informed of a proclamation commanding the party to disperse and denouncing them as rebels. Bacon disregarded the threat and proceeded to the outskirts of Richmond where he routed the redskins who retired to the western part of the state. This was the first act of the drama of the Virginia rebellion which was soon to lead to the burning of

Jamestown and the flight of Governor Berkeley across
Chesapeake Bay to Eastern Accomack.

BACON RECANTS

Bacon soon became the popular idol of the countryside
and was elected a Burgess in spite of the stigma of being
denounced as a rebel. When he went to the capital to take
his seat he was arrested and again branded as a rebel. After
a talk with the Governor he decided that it was expedient
to avoid open resistance and gave his word to obey a
parole. Although Jamestown was filled with the new Burgesses who sympathized with Bacon's ideas, he decided
that it was the wisest course for him to make a public re-
cantation which he did at the bar of the Assembly. But his
humility did not last long. After several days of quiet, he
heard that he was again in disfavor and that his arrest was
imminent. He took leave of the town a few hours before
he was sought by the authorities.

In a few days Bacon returned to Jamestown at the head
of 600 armed men. He demanded a commission and after
making threatening gestures was appointed General and
Commander-in-Chief against the Indians. A pardon was
granted to him and his followers who had defeated the
Susquehannocks. Again he heard that the Governor had
declared him to be a rebel. It had now become a personal
feud between a popular leader of the people and the vacil-
lating representative of the King.

One of the most significant events of the time was the
taking of an oath by Bacon's men, on the present site of
Williamsburg, to defend the colony against any of the
King's forces that might be sent from England to support Berkeley. This oath resembled in some respects the
Declaration of Independence signed at Philadelphia one
hundred years later.

From the Painting by Howard Pyle. (c) Harper & Brothers
NATHANIEL BACON AND HIS FOLLOWERS BURNING JAMESTOWN
From Vol. 2, "History of the American People" by Woodrow Wilson

Collapse of Rebellion when Bacon Dies

Governor Berkeley had assembled a party of a thousand men and returned to Jamestown. Bacon immediately marched on the capital and soon defeated the forces defending the town, caused Berkeley again to flee and burned the buildings so "that the rogues should harbor there no more." The end of the Rebellion came suddenly with the death of Bacon. He had contracted a fever in the trenches before Jamestown. There was no leader with ability or courage enough to carry forward the resistance to royal authority and secure the reforms demanded by Bacon. This defiance of oppressive rule ended with no practical results except to bring out into the open the abuses which were later to lead all the colonies to join in united rebellion against these same restrictive controls.

Unlike New England, where differences with the Crown and Governors did not lead to armed resistance, Virginia thus experienced an uprising or revolution where elemental features of democracy clearly were outlined and future developments presaged. Bacon's Rebellion in the light of later research has been considered a distinct movement towards American democracy, being frankly a contest between the people and the Royal Government.

FRENCH AND ENGLISH RELATIONS

While the settlers in the North American Colonies actively were concerned in establishing themselves and protecting their homes and villages against the Indians, strained relations between France and England were developing, due not only to colonization problems but to political events in the larger realm of European politics. These controversies led to conditions which to a greater or lesser extent also affected the English colonies in North America. The resulting wars or their repercussions continued intermittently until 1763, when the Peace of Paris sealed the triumph of the British and Colonial arms and settled the undisputed dominion of England over Canada and Newfoundland.

For over a century problems of exploration, settlements, fisheries, and commerce developed of special interest to the colonists, while the larger aspect of their circumstances was realized by both France and England. Occasional attention was paid to the situation of the provinces but a lack of any definite policy of colonization consistently followed on the part of either nation was evident. From time to time grants were made as uncertain in scope as they were incapable of being guaranteed and naturally these were affected by current European politics.

Colonies in America Become Involved

The Treaty of St. Germain in 1632 ceded Nova Scotia and Canada to France, and this may be said to mark the formal beginning of intermittent hostilities that involved the English colonies in greater or less participation in military operations by the settlers of the New World. Furthermore there were from time to time what turned out to be but temporary adjustments by various treaties negotiated to terminate wars where American interests were but minor elements to the signatories. Thus, after various conflicts, in 1654 an expedition sent by Cromwell conquered Nova Scotia, and in 1656 it was granted to Etienne de la Tour who transferred his allegiance from France to England. He later sold his lands and property to Sir Thomas Temple who started to develop the country.

In the interval between this activity and the Treaty of Breda, French colonization was active in Canada and was resisted by the English when the settlements came too close and threatened New England and New York. Such attempts in the western region of New York in 1656-1658 were broken up, but in 1665, with the arrival of Courcelle as Governor of New France, came an active period of French colonization marked also by energetic missionary enterprises of the Jesuits. There were expeditions against unfriendly Indians by both French and English, and a century of what might be termed colonial wars was well under way broken by periods of peace and treaties that so far as North America was concerned were in no way conclusive.

Acadia Restored to France

The Treaty of Breda ended the short war that had broken out in 1666 between England and France. There was an adjustment of territory, England restoring Acadia to France, and England receiving from that country Antigua, Montserrat, and St. Christopher in the West Indies.

Nevertheless the activity of the French in North America continued with ever growing intensity and relations with the Indians were cultivated, marked by a peace concluded between that country and the Five Nations. Ever moving westward the important trading post of Saulte Ste. Marie at the entrance of Lake Superior was founded by Pablon and Marquette, the latter continuing his exploration to discover the Mississippi in 1673.

In 1672 Count Frontenac (1620-1698) was appointed Governor of the French possessions in North America, and undertook with vigor settlement and exploration which greatly strengthened the position of that country. In 1673 he completed a fort at Ontario which he named after himself and also had a fort built at Michillimachinac at the head of Lake Huron. While these movements did not actually involve the English colonists in hostilities yet they may be mentioned here as indicating what was a most serious development laying the foundation for the strife between England and France in the new world, in which the colonists were considerably more than spectators.

PORTRAIT AND SIGN-MANUAL OF KING PHILIP

From Vol. 2, "History of the American People" by Woodrow Wilson

KING PHILIP'S WAR

One of the early and most important of the organized efforts at defence of the New England Colonies came as the result of various Indian attacks and outrages under Philip of Pokanoket, the son of Massasoit, chief of the Wampanoag tribe and head of a league that included Indians from Maine to Connecticut.

In 1675 in the Rhode Island and Plymouth colonies such attacks became serious, and at Swansea near the Rhode Island boundary settlers were killed and houses burned. On June 24, 1675, an attack was made on the colonists in this town as they were returning to their homes after a Fast Day service. This and other outbreaks marked the beginning of what came to be known as King Philip's War. Immediately the colonies of Plymouth and Massachusetts Bay united with Rhode Island, and later were joined by Connecticut, in placing in the field organized troops, convinced that the time had arrived for drastic effective measures. Accordingly war was undertaken in earnest and continued until the Great Swamp Fight of December 19, 1675 and the death of Philip in the next year removed this menace from the settlers.

Colonists Unite against Indians

The Great Swamp Fight, involving as did the largest force of colonists operating as a united military body, has been celebrated by the Society of Colonial Wars in the State of New York as the date of its General Court. In fact the first of these annual celebrations was held after the organization of the Society in 1892 and the important address of the evening was delivered by Nathan G. Pond, one of the founders of the Society, on "The Great Swamp Fight in 1675."

The Great Swamp Fight was described also in a paper read before the Society of Colonial Wars in the State of New York December 19, 1903, by a member, Hamilton B. Tompkins, Esq., and printed in full in a volume of Addresses published by the Society, Publication No. 13, in 1907.

It may be of interest to quote from this paper a summary of this operation.

"King Philip's War, as such, commenced by the attack of the Indians upon the inhabitants of Swanzey, Massachusetts, as they were returning from church on the 20th of June, 1675, which was followed by attacks upon the towns of Dartmouth, Taunton, and Middleborough. On the 15th of July of the same year, the Commissioners of Massachusetts and Connecticut, attended by a strong military force, were sent to the Narragansetts to obtain new guarantees of friendship. They succeeded in negotiating a treaty by which the chiefs of that powerful tribe agreed, for a stipulated price, to deliver to the English, living or dead, whatever subjects of Philip should come within their country, and to resist any invasion of their own lands or those of the English, and gave hostages for their fulfillment of these engagements. The Indian War continued . . . with attacks upon Brookfield and the Connecticut River towns of Hadley, Hatfield, Deerfield, and others.

FEAR OF THE NARRAGANSETTS

"In September, the Commissioners of the United Colonies, Massachusetts, Plymouth, and Connecticut, which formed the confederacy, met at Boston, and decided to raise a thousand men for a defensive war; that of this force Massachusetts was to furnish 527, Connecticut 315, and Plymouth 158. In October, the attitude of the formidable Narragansetts was regarded with anxiety, as it was known that so far from keeping their compact, made in July, they had harbored many of Philip's dispersed allies. Canonchet and other chiefs came to Boston while the Commissioners were in session, and promised that the hostile Indians, whom they admitted were under their protection, should be surrendered within ten days. The time arrived, but no Indians appeared. The Commissioners became alarmed; if the strongest and most numerous of the New England tribes, the Narragansetts, were to prove faithless, and should commence active hostilities, great, indeed, would be the peril of the colonists. The fifth day after the breach of the treaty, the Commissioners reassembled, and determined that, besides the number of soldiers formerly agreed upon to be raised, one thousand more should be provided and forwarded for service in the Narragansett country. Governor Winslow was appointed Chief and the Colony of Connecticut was to furnish the second in command. Major Robert Treat was subsequently chosen for this place. The commander was to put himself at the head of his forces within six weeks, and in the meantime 'a solemn day of humiliation and prayer' was kept throughout the confederacy.

"In giving notice of their action to the several General Courts or Colonies, the Commissioners commended That care be taken that the soldiers sent on the expedition be men of courage, strength, and activity, their arms well fixed for service; that their clothing be in all respects strong and

warm, suitable for the season; that they have provisions in
their knapsacks for a week's march from their rendezvous;
and also that there be a number of ministers and chirur-
geons provided and appointed for the expedition.' . . .

PREPARING FOR INDIAN WARFARE

"Early in December the Colonial troops commenced to
gather. There were six companies from Massachusetts, under the command of Major Appleton and Captains Mosely,
Gardner, Davenport, Oliver, and Johnson; from Connecticut, five companies, under Major Treat and Captains See-
ley, Gallup, Mason, Watts and Marshall; two companies
from Plymouth, under Major Bradford and Captain Gor-
ham. Captain Benjamin Church was invited by Governor
Winslow to command a company; he declined taking a
commission, but promised to accompany the expedition as
a volunteer. Attached to the levy from Connecticut were
some Mohegan Indians; but they did not render any substantial aid in the fight which followed.

"On the 12th of December, most of the army arrived
at Mr. Smith's in Wickford, the place intended for their
headquarters. 'Captain Mosely on his way thither,' says
Hubbard, 'had happily surprised thirty Indians, one of
whom he took along with him as a guide. Peter by name,
who, under some disgust with his countrymen, or his
Sachem, which made him prove the more real friend to our
forces, wherein he faithfully performed what he promised;
and without his assistance our men would have been much
at loss to have found the enemy until it had been too late
to have fought them:' . . .

"On the 15th, Bull's Garrison House, in South Kings-
town, at what is now known as Tower Hill, intended for
a place of shelter, had been attacked by the Indians and
demolished. At Pettaquanscutt, where shelter was also

From the Collection of The Ancient and Honorable Artillery Company

TREATY WITH KING PHILIP

(The Indian is shown wearing a Western headress)

expected, it was found that the Indians had destroyed the buildings and butchered the inhabitants.

"Some of the troops were a little late, but on the 18th the various forces were united, and the whole army encamped in the open air, the weather being cold and snowy. The next day, upon setting out, Captains Mosely and Davenport led the van; Major Appleton and Captain Oliver followed; General Winslow and the Plymouth forces held the centre; and the Connecticut contingent brought up the rear. Captain Oliver, in his account, says: 'In the morning, December 19th, Lord's Day, at five o'clock, we marched; snow two or three feet deep, and withal an extreme hard frost, so that some of our men were frozen in their hands and feet, and thereby disabled from service'" . . .

THE GREAT SWAMP FIGHT

"The stronghold of the Narragansetts, fifteen miles away, was reached at one o'clock. The fort, which the Indians had fortified to the best of their ability, was on a solid piece of upland, encompassed by a swamp. In it were gathered according to the best authorities, about thirty-five hundred Indians. On the inner side of this natural defence they had driven rows of palisades, encircled about with a hedge nearly a rod in thickness; and the only entrance to the enclosure was by a fallen tree or log, four or five feet from the ground, this bridge being protected by a block house right over 'against it, from which,' says Hubbard, 'they sorely galled our men that first went in.'

"In spite of the fact that the English were wearied by their long march through the snow, scarcely halting to refresh themselves with food, immediately upon arriving they commenced the onset. The colonists had been so long in making their preparations that the Indians were well apprised of their approach, and had made the best

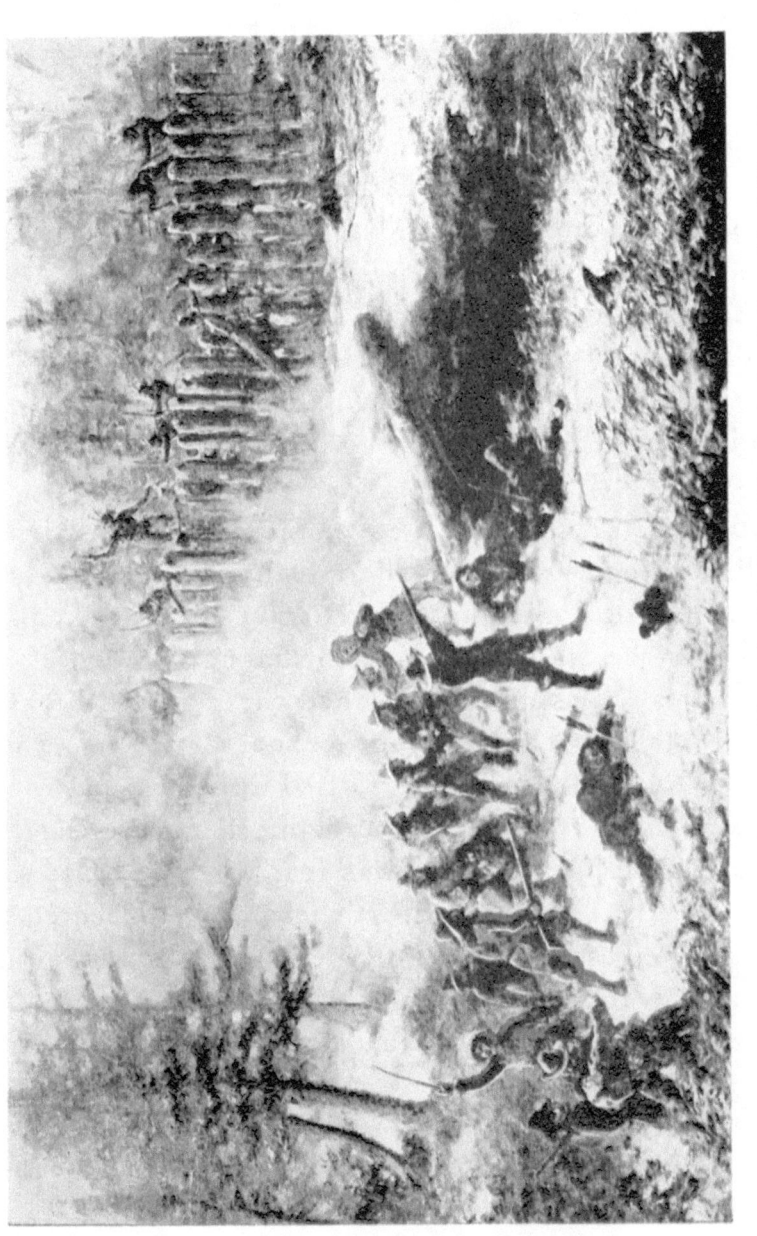

THE GREAT SWAMP FIGHT AT KINGSTON, R. I., 1675

From Vol. 6, "The Pageant of America"

arrangements in their power to withstand them. The beginning was most disastrous to the officers. Captain Johnson, of Roxbury, was shot dead on the bridge as he was rushing over at the head of his company. Captain Davenport, of Boston, had succeeded in penetrating within the enclosure, when he met the same fate. Captain Gardner, of Salem, and two of the Connecticut captains, Gallup, of New London, and Marshall, of Windsor, were also killed outright, while Lieutenant Upham, of Boston, and Captain Seely, of Stratford, received wounds which afterwards proved fatal. Major Bradford, of Plymouth, was sorely wounded, as well as Captain John Mason, or Norwich, and Captain Benjamin Church.

Indian Fort Captured and Village Burned

"Notwithstanding the fall of their leaders, the rank and file pressed on, and although the entrance was choked by the bodies of the slain, yet over the mangled corpses of their comrades the assailants climbed the logs and breastworks in their efforts to penetrate the fort. Once they were beaten out, but they soon rallied and regained their ground. The conflict raged with varying success for nearly three hours. . . . The carnage was fearful; the result was yet doubtful; until an entrance to the fort was effected in the rear by the reserve guard of the Connecticut troops. The Indians, who were all engaged at the first point of attack, were surprised and confused by a heavy fire behind them; their powder was nearly consumed; but their arrows continued to rain a deadly shower upon the charging foe. The wigwams were set on fire within the fort, contrary to the earnest entreat of Captain Church, who, with his knowledge of military matters and the condition of the assailants, realized the importance of shelter and food to the exhausted conquerors. . . . 'Humanity and policy alike,' continues Arnold, 'sustained the advice of the gallant

Church, but it was too late. The infuriated colonists had
already commenced the work of destruction; in a few min-
utes the frail material of five hundred Indian dwellings
furnished the funeral pyre of the wounded and dying; the
blazing homes of the Narragansetts lighted their path to
death.'

"More than a thousand of the enemy perished. The English lost, in killed and wounded, according to Hubbard,
over two hundred; and other accounts place the numbers
still higher. A large portion of these might have been saved
if the advice of Church had been followed. When night
fell there was no shelter or provisions for the conquerors
or conquered. . . .

"They (The English) had now to retrace their steps in
the dark, through a dense forest, with a deep snow beneath
their feet and a December storm howling about their heads.
By the glare of the burning wigwams they formed their
line of march back to Wickford, bearing with them their
dead and wounded, 'a march,' says Cotton Mather, 'made
through hardships that an whole age could not parallel.' It
was two o'clock before they reached the camping ground.
The cold was severe; many died on the way; the limbs of
the wounded were stiffened; and fatigue had disabled most
of the remainder. There was no shelter or provisions of any
sort, and when morning dawned it was found that death
had done a melancholy work. . . .

"After the Great Swamp Fight the sick and wounded
were carried to the Island of Rhode Island, where they were
cared for by the people of Portsmouth and Newport. . . .

Power Of Indians Broken

"This virtually ended the expedition, and the 'Great
Swamp Fight,' most memorable in New England history
and the annals of the early colonists. The power of
the Narragansetts was irretrievably broken; the survivors

returned the next day to their smouldering and ruined fort, and found some provisions to ameliorate their starving condition. It was fortunate that the Indians had been too dazed by their defeat to pursue their retreating foes, or the remnant of the English army would have been destroyed; and this course, says Mather, had been advised by some of the leaders of the Narragansetts. . . .

"After their disastrous defeat, we hear of but little more of the Narragansetts. The remainder submitted the following year, and gradually diminishing in numbers, they never again became formidable as a race, or offered any organized resistance to the colonists."

With the termination of King Philip's War in 1676, the American Colonies underwent for a while various vicissitudes, more political than those involving military activities. Notwithstanding European disturbances organized warfare was not brought directly to the colonists. Bacon's Rebellion, already noticed, the dispute over the boundaries of Massachusetts and New Hampshire with the establishment of the latter as a Crown Colony in 1680, the establishment of Pennsylvania 1680-1682, the controversy between Massachusetts and the Crown, resulting in the forfeiture of the Charter, October 13, 1684, the loss of certain liberties by Connecticut and Carolina in 1680, followed by similar action in Maryland, all were activities preliminary to the Revolution in England and the accession of William and Mary to the throne, February 13, 1689.

English Colonists Cleared Land for Farms

The re-establishment of various colonial governments in North America and the incidental political confusion in New England militated against adequate and organized defence of which the Indians, even where not encouraged by the French, were only too ready to take advantage. It should be remembered in connection with the Indians that the French from the very outset had shown far more tact in their relations with them than had the English.

One fundamental difference that can be emphasized was the desire of the French that the Indians should remain as hunters and trappers for the furtherance of the fur trade, while the English sought to clear the lands they took possession of for agriculture and the establishment of a rural civilization of denser population.

KING WILLIAM'S WAR

Naturally Indian attacks were of importance and distress to the colonists, but more serious and extended hostilities came when war was declared against France in April 1689, by England. This was a universal war against Louis XIV, known in America as King William's War and prosecuted vigorously at home and abroad until the Peace of Ryswick, September 20, 1697, between France, England, Spain, and Holland, which acknowledged William III as King of England and Anne as his successor.

Accordingly in this war the North American continent became the scene of active hostilities with the Canadian Indians and those of Maine assisting the French and receiving from them arms and munitions, while the Iroquois sided with the English. Frankly it might be said that the English Colonists were more directly concerned with the fortunes of the home land when war was brought directly to their own doors with military operations against France and Spain extending from Canada to Florida, rather than in undertaking any distant offensive operations on their own account in behalf of the mother country.

FRENCH AND INDIANS ATTACK NORTHERN NEW YORK
The year 1690 witnessed three important and shocking catastrophes for the colonists in surprise attacks and

destruction of Schenectady (February 8, 1690), Salmon
Falls (March 18, 1690), and Casco (May 17, 1690), by
organized bands of French and Indians. The various colonies now united in a plan for a main offensive against
Canada which strategically was entirely sound, but for its
execution there was lacking not only competent leadership and organization, but an unwillingness to sink petty
jealousies and present a united front to the enemy. One
serious result of the political difficulties had been a disbanding of the colonial forces collected and organized by
Andros the Royal Governor, and but feeble attempts were
made to secure joint troops from the various colonies to
act against the Indians in Maine, New Hampshire, and
northern Massachusetts. One of these expeditions was
under the command of Colonel Benjamin Church, a leader
in King Philip's War, but little was accomplished.

The opening event of colonial military effort in King
William's War was the expedition of Sir William Phips
against Port Royal, which sailed from Nantasket, Boston
Harbor, on April 28, 1690, in five ships with a force of
several hundred. This Nova Scotia fort, with its small garrison outnumbered, soon surrendered, May 11, 1690, and
the colonists gathered their plunder. A Congress of the
colonies of Massachusetts, Plymouth, and New York voted
for a combined expedition against Canada and this was the
first instance of the Americans acting together in a formal
undertaking against a common foreign enemy.

CANADA TO BE ATTACKED

Here was planned a joint movement with a land force
marching from Albany to attack Montreal and a fleet from
Boston to move against Quebec. The plan was of interest as the movement was essayed by the colonies without
proper preparation and without consultation with the

English Government. The land expedition was inadequately organized and equipped, and lacking the quotas
of troops promised by the colonies involved, met with
difficulties from the outset. A dispute over the position
of joint commander, lack of suitable equipment, and an
almost entire incapacity to carry on such an expedition,
among other causes, led to its collapse and somewhat
ignominious return after it had reached Wood Creek near
the southern end of Lake Champlain. This futile attempt
clearly showed the inability of the colonies at that time to
organize for successful co-operative military action independent of England, and emphasized the inadequacy of the
strength of men and of equipment they could assemble.

The sea expedition against Quebec which left Boston
on August 9, 1690, in some thirty-two vessels of various
sorts and sizes, and aggregating some 2200 men, while it
reached its destination was hardly more successful. Various delays enabled reinforcements under Frontenac to
reach Quebec which was able to resist siege from a landing
force and bombardment by the fleet. Not only was there
lack of success in gaining the objective but the troops
suffered from disease and exposure, while the cost of the
expedition almost bankrupted the Colony of Massachusetts Bay. Again this costly demonstration of the incompetence of the leaders for such an enterprise outside of
their own boundaries, showed that, notwithstanding the
bravery of the land forces under Major John Walley, no
measure of success against a foe well organized and led
could be expected in the absence of trained commanders
and disciplined and seasoned troops.

In Europe the defeat of James II by William of Orange
at the battle of the Boyne in Ireland, July 1, 1690, decided
that England was to be a Protestant country, but in the
New World outside of the constant rivalry between French

and English colonies religious animosities were not such as to develop resort to arms.

Peace Brings No Territorial Change

The war continued without notable activity in North America until the Peace of Ryswick, September 30, 1697. Here, with the mutual restoration of conquered positions and lands between France and England and Holland, there were no territorial changes. In 1690 it was stated that there were about 215,000 English as compared with some 12,000 French in North America, but in addition to circumstances elsewhere mentioned the French were better organized for war and always enjoyed invaluable support from the Indians.

Typical of the desire for protection was the construction of Fort William Henry at Pemaquid by Sir William Phips in 1692, but in 1696 it was captured by the French under Iberville. The year 1693 marked the first of a series of expeditions against the Iroquois, loyal to the English, under Count Frontenac, who, appointed Governor of the French possessions in North America, was recalled to France in 1682, but returned to Canada in 1689, where he had a distinguished career until his death at Quebec in 1698.

The Peace of Ryswick negotiated in September 1697 was the beginning of a brief peace of but five years, but at this time there were many important economic and political events.

On October 13, 1684, Massachusetts lost its charter which had been a subject of controversy for many years and occasioned serious differences between that colony and the Crown and Parliament. While this event did not have any serious military repercussions, yet it marked an important political development in the colonies leading to a readjustment of relations with the home government.

In more than one of the colonies the result was materially to change such relations in the direction of the restriction of rights and liberties which had grown up with tacit acceptance by English ministries yet without special recognition. This was especially true when political concerns in Britain required the entire attention of government and ministries.

With the sending of royal governors to the colonies there began to develop chains of circumstances that laid the foundations for the inevitable movement for independence and liberty which characterized the eighteenth century. Nevertheless these matters in the main involved internal economies and politics and did not affect military efforts by the provincial settlers either in the measures of defense against the Indians or in the European wars that were brought to the New World.

QUEEN ANNE'S WAR

On May 4, 1702, shortly after Anne ascended the throne of England on the death of William III (March 8, 1702), war was declared on France by the Grand Alliance, comprising England, the Holy Roman Empire under Leopold III, a claimant for the throne of Spain, Prussia, and later by Portugal and Savoy. This war, known in Europe as the War of the Spanish Succession, usually is referred to in America as Queen Anne's War from the name of the reigning monarch. In this war England began to recognize its relations to her American Colonies by sending naval expeditions to their aid. The first hostility in the New World where the now familiar pattern of the attacks by French and Indians of King William's War was the Deerfield Massacre of 1704, when that Massachusetts town was destroyed. This incident in part was avenged by Colonel Benjamin Church, who had figured in King Philip's War, by moving against the French settlements on the New England Coast. Another serious massacre was that at Haverhill in 1708 when French and Indians attacked that town and killed 16 and captured 35 of the inhabitants.

INVASION OF SOUTHERN COLONIES
Passing for the moment to the Southern colonies, not always thought of so prominently in connection with

colonial wars as those of New England mention might be made of the invasion of Carolina and an attack on Charleston in 1706 by French and Spanish forces from Florida. This was partly in assertion of Spanish territorial claims to that colony as a part of Florida. Both land and sea attacks were repulsed and defeated by William Rhett. The St. Augustine government stirred up the frontier tribes against the English. These southern attacks aroused a common interest with the New England colonies.

Of special interest to the American Colonies were various expeditions against the French settlements on New Foundland and in Canada, with their opportunities for fisheries and the fur trade. New England demanded the expulsion of the French from Acadia and the capture of the French fortress at Port Royal. In 1704 the Colonists assembled a fleet at Boston Harbor for such a purpose, while in 1707 an unsuccessful colonial expedition attempted its conquest. However, England now becoming alive to colonial acquisitions of territory in the New World, in 1709 determined on bringing Canada, Acadia, and New Foundland under its control. An English fleet was to be sent to America and some 27,000 colonial troops were to be enlisted against Quebec and Montreal. While this project was abandoned by the English Government, huge debts were incurred by Connecticut, New York, and New Jersey, which were forced to issue paper money.

Capture of Port Royal

In 1710 under the command of Sir Francis Nicholson (1660-1728), an English Colonial Governor, a fleet of six English and thirty vessels from New England sailing from Boston in September with four New England regiments, demanded the surrender of Port Royal which, inadequately garrisoned, capitulated. The name was changed to Annapolis after Queen Anne.

After this success there was organized in the following year, a greater expedition against Quebec under command of Sir Hovenden Walker. This comprised fifteen men of war, forty transports, seven regiments from Marlborough's victorious army, and a battalion of marines, in addition to forces raised by the colonies, the whole aggregating 6463 soldiers, assembling in June and July at Boston. The colonists also contributed a considerable army from Connecticut, New Jersey, and New York, organized to attack Montreal. Both expeditions failed of accomplishment, the former meeting with serious disaster and shipwreck, requiring its abandonment. While the colonists participated actively in this war the net results were but meagre.

In Europe notable British victories won by Marlborough at Blenheim (August 13, 1704) and at Ramillies (May 23, 1706), together with that of Prince Eugene of Savoy at Turin (September 7, 1706), and successes by Marlborough at Oudenarde (July 11, 1708) and Malplaquet (September 11, 1709), as well as political developments and dissension among the allies brought about the Peace of Utrecht (April 11, 1713). England had captured Gibraltar from Spain (July 24, 1704) and there were changes of boundaries of European countries as well as of colonies, but in North America eleven years of war had produced few important changes. France ceded to England: New Foundland, Nova Scotia (Acadia), and Hudson Bay Territory. Most significant, however, was a more or less serious attempt at unity among the English colonies in North America, which frankly was not only difficult to develop but, notwithstanding its obvious necessity, was slow in its realization.

FLORIDA ATTACKED BY CAROLINA MILITIA

When the War of the Spanish Succession (Queen Anne's War) broke out, James Moore, Governor of South Carolina, led a force invading Florida against St. Augustine, but retreated burning two of his ships when the Spanish frigates appeared. In 1706 Charleston was attacked by a French and Spanish squadron. However, the Carolina militia drove off a landing party before it secured lodgement. The French withdrew and another expedition proved disastrous for them.

North and South Carolina were divided in 1710 and the following year, September 22-24, 1711, there was a massacre of Carolina settlers at New Bern by the Tuscarora Indians. This led to an active campaign headed by Col. John Barnwell resulting in all but annihilation for these savages. Again in 1715 the Yamassees, the Creeks, Catawbas, and Cherokees, instigated by the Spaniards at St. Augustine, undertook hostilities against the colonists at various settlements, but a year later were defeated by Governor Craven and driven from South Carolina to Florida across the Spanish border to the south. In 1718 in the war between England and Spain the Spaniards planned an expedition against Charleston.

Returning to the north, it was becoming increasingly apparent that as settlements developed in Western New York the rapid growth of the fur trade and the activity of the French were becoming serious considerations for the province. It was realized by William Burnet, the Royal Governor of New York and New Jersey from 1720 to 1728, that the French were seeking to hem in on the west the English Colonies as they expanded their settlements and trade in that direction. To offset this tendency he established at Oswego on Lake Ontario, at the mouth of the river of that name, a trading post, the first English centre of this nature on the Great Lakes. This was destined to become an important centre of Indian trade and was fortified in 1726 much to the annoyance of the French. The latter were loath to attack it, though they sought to have it destroyed by friendly Indians.

This post of Oswego was destined to play a more or less important part later in the French and Indian War. In the meantime the English sought to carry on negotiations with the Six Nations of the Iroquois Confederacy to which the Tuscaroras recently had been admitted. In the main the relations of the English with the Indians were not on as sound a basis or as skillfully conducted as were those of the French with whom the red men became in many cases valuable allies both in military affairs and in trade developments.

For a number of years it would have been sound policy for the various English Colonies to have united to resist French aggression, but too often boundary disputes and local jealousies interfered with any united action and a firm front to their neighbors to the north. It must be remembered that when the French founded either a trading post or a military outpost it functioned in both relations, and in addition to strategic importance its value as a centre for the fur trade was never lost sight of.

In New England the rapid extension of settlements by colonists ever seeking new and better tracts of land inevitably brought them into conflict with the Indians, who were encouraged by the French to hostilities against the English settlers. In 1724 came a war with the Abenaki tribe which for a time resisted such aggression by attacking outlying settlements. The colonists retaliated and in a series of savage conflicts forced the Abenakis to withdraw to Canada or to live in peace, accepting the supremacy of the White Men.

KING GEORGE'S WAR

From 1739 to 1748 Great Britain was at war with Spain and in the attendant hostilities the American Colonies participated in poorly planned and badly executed campaigns. This conflict was known in Europe as the War of the Austrian Succession and in America as King George's War. It may be divided into, first, the Spanish operations, and then, after 1744 when France declared war on England, into expeditions against Canada on a large scale by the English and troops from their New England colonies.

From the time of the purchase of Georgia by the British government in 1730 and its establishment as a colony by charter in 1732, problems of colonization and administration were more conspicuous than military activity, especially after the landing of James Oglethorpe in 1732. Nevertheless the danger of Spanish invasion was realized, compulsory military service was required and fortifications were built. In the Spanish war in 1739 troops from Georgia served as a bulwark.

Oglethorpe Attacks St. Augustine

In 1740 Oglethorpe led 1200 men from Georgia along with men from Carolina and Virginia, against the Spaniards in Florida, laying siege to St. Augustine in an unsuccessful expedition. In the same year Admiral Edward Vernon, who in 1739 had captured Porto Bello, commanded an expedition of 27,000 men directed against Carthagena in which the colonies north of Carolina contributed four battalions. This accomplished nothing of importance owing to the ravages of disease. Again in 1741 American colonials took part in an expedition against Cuba but no results were scored.

The attacks of the English and their provincial troops in the West Indies were returned in the following year (1742), when the Spaniards landing in Georgia to attack the forts on the Altamaha River were repulsed and defeated at Frederica by Oglethorpe with a loss of some 3000.

In 1742 England had formed an alliance with Austria, a state that now was opposed by France, Bavaria, and Spain, and later by Saxony and Prussia. On March 20, 1744, France declared war on England, but so far as the European conflict and the invasion of England by the Pretender (Bonnie Prince Charlie), little enthusiasm or even interest was aroused in the American Colonies. However, in May 1744 came an overt act in the surprise attack by the French on the English garrison at Canso, destroying the fishing station, fort, and other buildings and capturing eighty men who were removed to Louisbourg as prisoners. This occurred before the declaration of war was received in New England, and aroused the colonists.

DECISION TO ATTACK LOUISBOURG

The immediate result was the determination of William Shirley, Governor of Massachusetts, to reduce and capture Louisbourg, and thus remove a menace to the New England fisheries as well as a strong military and naval base. The expedition duly was authorized by the Legislature of Massachusetts, by one vote, and was approved by the King. Accordingly in the following year, April 30 to June 16, 1745, William Pepperrell, a Maine merchant of Kittery,

From the Painting by F. Luis Mora.   (c) Harper & Brothers

OGLETHORPE'S EXPEDITION AGAINST ST. AUGUSTINE, 1740

From Vol. 3, "History of the American People", by Woodrow Wilson

at the head of 4000 Colonial troops laid siege to this fortress which shared with Quebec the distinction of being the strongest military post in North America. The Colonial troops were drawn from Maine, New Hampshire, Vermont, Connecticut, and included fishermen, mechanics, and farmers. For once there was harmony, not only among the soldiers from the different colonies and among their commanding officers, but between them and the forces of the Crown and their leaders. A few English vessels of war participated in the expedition which resulted in a notable triumph for the Colonial arms.

CAPTURE OF LOUISBOURG

The Society of Colonial Wars has printed many interesting and scholarly papers on the Siege of Louisbourg and its capture. From one of the volumes, *Louisbourg Journals* (New York, 1932), edited by Louis Effingham de Forest, M.A., J.D., may be quoted the "Historical Introduction" as it summarizes concisely this notable siege. It is essentially as follows:

"The capture of Louisbourg in 1745 was the most important military achievement of the American Colonists prior to the War of the Revolution and, in fact, the only British success of any importance during the entire War of the Austrian Succession. It was an amazing victory and had a profound effect on the spirit and temper of the times.

New Military Power Arises

"Parkman called the expedition a 'mad scheme' and 'a project of wild audacity,' and used these terms with justification. The expedition was planned by Governor Shirley, a lawyer, entirely ignorant of the art of war, who even gave directions in advance as to just how and when the fort was to be taken by surprise. It was commanded by a rich merchant, William Pepperrell, who had seen only a brief and uneventful service in the militia. The army was composed of farmers, fishermen, shopkeepers, and artisans, with no

From the Collection of the Society of Colonial Wars

VIEW OF THE LANDING OF NEW ENGLAND FORCES IN EXPEDITION
AGAINST CAPE BRETON, 1745

conception of discipline. They went to face the regulars of the standing army of the first military power of Europe, protected by the walls of one of the great fortresses of the day. When Louisbourg fell the civilized world recognized that a new military power had risen in America. As for the Americans it gave them a confidence in themselves which they never lost. At Bunker Hill where the patriots' fortifications were laid out by Richard Gridley, who was an artillery officer at Louisbourg, the. Americans laughed at the earthworks of the British and compared them to the great walls of the citadel on Cape Breton. . . .

"France considered the possession of Louisbourg absolutely necessary to the control of her Canadian possessions. Holding that excellent harbor of Cape Breton, which was easily defended, she could command the entrance to the gulf and river St. Lawrence and have a clear port for imports as well as exports. Thus actuated, France spent a sum equivalent today to ten million dollars in erecting a fortress which would be impregnable. Under the shelter of Louisbourg's great guns rode a large fleet of ships which was a constant menace to all of New England. When France declared war the garrison at Louisbourg, supported by the French fleet, threatened to exterminate entirely the fisheries which were the foundation of New England's maritime trade.

"For these reasons the desire to capture Louisbourg long was close to the hearts of the people of New England. The impulse to take active offensive measures came with the arrival of the news at Boston in 1744 that the garrison was small, the Swiss contingent mutinous, and the French discontented, and that there was a scarcity of supplies. . . .

AUDACITY BRINGS SUCCESS

"Parkman wrote that the triumph was 'the result of mere audacity and hardihood, backed by the rarest good luck' and this seems a reasonable statement. Fortune surely favored the English. In the first place the weather was perfect. Every sail arrived at Canso harbor and for forty-seven days the army enjoyed ideal fighting conditions in a country notable for storms. Secondly, the work of repair being done on the Grand Battery just at this time made it necessary for the French to abandon what was normally a strong fort. The rashness of the commander of the French relief ship, the *Vigilant,* led to its unnecessary capture. These events, with the mutinous spirit of the French garrison and the lack of pay and supplies, undoubtedly greatly assisted the vigorous attack.

"There should not be overlooked the presence of Commodore Peter Warren, an able officer, with an effective fleet. Warren and Pepperell were, fortunately, men of tact and patience and the difficulties of a joint command shared by a British naval officer and a Provincial militia general were never permitted to interfere with the purposes of the operations."

The American colonists greatly encouraged by their success at Louisbourg and elated at their accomplishment now projected a conquest of Canada in which all the northern colonies would join. Shirley and Warren made ambitious plans to that end, while in England the Duke of Newcastle ordered extensive preparations for imperial co-operation. A Colonial army of more than 8000 men was proposed and naval aid from England was counted on. On the other hand the French planned the recovery of Louisbourg and a large fleet under D'Anville arrived at Nova Scotia, but failed of accomplishing anything due to the death of its commander, an epidemic of pestilence, and the loss of ships in a storm. The promised fleet from England did not arrive and little further was accomplished by the colonists, as the French were not even driven from their posts in Nova Scotia.

From the Collection of The New York Historical Society

GENERAL PEPPERRELL COMMANDING COLONIAL FORCES AT
SIEGE OF LOUISBOURG, 1745

In 1747 a French fleet with troops destined for Canada and Nova Scotia was encountered by Anson and Warren and forced to strike its colors. The American colonists suffered in border attacks by French and Indians but little of their ambitious plans were realized, and in this year the Duke of Newcastle ordered the disbanding of the army that was being organized for an American campaign.

UNITY OF COLONIES DEVELOPS

Aside from military operations this period marked the development of a consciousness of unity, not only among the colonists of English stock but among the other settlers along the Atlantic seaboard. There was growing a feeling of strength and independence and a departure from any slavish devotion to the country of origin in Europe. The Dutch, Swedes, Swiss, Huguenots, and others as well as the English shared this feeling. As a Swede traveler (Kalin) in America wrote in 1748, "Exceeding freedom and prosperity nurse an untamable spirit, but this condition the English Government and its military and naval officers sent to the Colonies fail utterly to realize." An instance of this was the resistance of the men of Boston, Massachusetts, in 1747 to the impressment of seamen for Royal ships of war.

An example of the growing feeling of unity was the proposal of Benjamin Franklin in 1747 that there should be a common militia and that the Colonies should be put on a defense basis. He advocated the construction of batteries on the Delaware River and that there should be raised at least 120 companies of militia, of which Philadelphia raised ten companies of about 100 men each.

King George's War terminated with the Treaty of Aix-la-Chapelle between England, France, and Spain, but it brought little satisfaction to the American colonists. There was reciprocal restoration of conquests by the signatories, and this unfortunately involved the restoration of Louisbourg to the French who received Cape Breton, while the English obtained Madras in India. This peace was of short duration for almost immediately disputes about boundaries sprang up between the French and English in which naturally the colonists with their growing commerce and maritime industries were vitally interested.

VIRGINIA TROOPS UNDER WASHINGTON

These disagreements as regards territory between the two countries were by no means confined to Eastern Canada and Newfoundland, but lands to the west of the settled English colonies now began to figure in counterclaims and disputes, particularly after exploration and establishment of trading posts. This was indeed the case with the great activity of the French explorers in the Great Lakes region, in the Mississippi Valley, and beyond the Appalachian Mountains. Governor Dinwiddie of the Colony of Virginia in 1753 dispatched Colonel George Washington to the forts on the Allegheny and Ohio rivers to remonstrate with the French on their encroachments. No immediate results were forthcoming and Virginia sent to the Ohio a colonial force of which two companies were commanded by Colonel Washington. Contact with a small French party in the advance upon Fort Du Quesne at the meeting of the Allegheny and Monongahela rivers led to its capture, but in turn the colonials were besieged in Fort Necessity built by Washington and were forced to capitulate.

The conference developed general discussion and debate rather than definite resolutions, but Franklin's plan of a confederation met with assent "pretty unanimous." At this time the Southern colonies did not enjoy such intimate relations with one another and with their neighbors to the north as were soon to develop and which figured so extensively at the time of the American Revolution.

RESUMPTION OF HOSTILITIES—
THE FRENCH AND INDIAN WAR

In fact many events and conditions arising after the Treaty of Aix-la-Chapelle indicated clearly a resumption of active hostilities on an even wider basis in America, as well as in Asia and Africa. Accordingly, to North America was sent General Braddock with an English army and a conference of colonial governors was held with the representatives of the Crown. Three expeditions in force were duly determined on, namely: (1) against Fort Du Quesne, (2) against Fort Niagara, and (3) against Crown Point in New York.

The first positive action of the war, which was not formally declared until the following year (1756), was the capture of Forts Beausejour and Gaspereaux in Nova Scotia (June 16-17, 1755) by a force of 3000 Massachusetts troops under Winslow and Monkton, and the consequent scattering of about 7000 of the inhabitants who refused to render allegiance to England, an episode celebrated in Longfellow's poem "Evangeline."

Other forts were taken by the English, and after various conferences the French inhabitants were transported from their homes which were destroyed. This established complete English sovereignty in Acadia though the chapter is not a particularly savory one in English colonial relations. The population thus removed was distributed during the remainder of the year among the English colonies to the south from New Hampshire to Georgia.

Braddock Leads English Forces

The expedition against Fort Du Quesne brought little of glory to the English arms, but it was important as marking an epoch in colonial affairs in North America bringing Virginia and the Southern colonies into close political co-operation with the Northern provinces. General Edward Braddock with two English regiments had arrived at Chesapeake Bay in February, 1755, to act as commander-in-chief of all the regular British and Provincial troops in America. In the following April he conferred with the Colonial Governors of Massachusetts, Virginia, New York, Maryland, Pennsylvania, and North Carolina, at Alexandria, Virginia.

Already Virginia had been aroused by the activity of the French from Canada who were proceeding down the Allegheny Valley and establishing military posts near the head waters of the Ohio River. By 1753 the situation for the Old Dominion was as acute as for the Northern colonies and Virginia now became vitally interested in what was clearly a continental struggle to determine whether France or England should rule North America. George Washington was sent by Governor Dinwiddie to negotiate with the Indian tribes and to warn the French not to invade English territory. The Great Meadows skirmish, July 3, 1754, represented the first overt act in the campaign that soon was to follow.

Battle of Fort Du Quesne

Definite plans were made for the expedition against Fort Du Quesne which was to be under the personal command of General Braddock, who, as soon as preliminary arrangements were completed, proceeded to the western border of

WASHINGTON RAISING THE BRITISH FLAG AT FORT DU QUESNE

Virginia and formed a camp at Fort Cumberland. Here the provincial militia which joined the army were collected for training according to the British system, and horses and wagons were assembled. Difficulties incident to starting a campaign in a newly settled country were many, and the English general was loath to take the advice of Benjamin Franklin and other colonial officials. By June the army had advanced westward, slowly building roads, and encumbered by much useless baggage. So slow was the progress that Colonel George Washington of the Virginia militia, now serving as aide to General Braddock, urged that officer to select an advance party of some 1200 men, chosen with lighter baggage and artillery, and leave the main army to make slower progress with the heavier wagons.

This advance detachment reached the Monongahela on July 8, 1755, at a point not far distant from Fort Du Quesne, which in the meantime had received substantial reinforcements of French and Indians. The river was duly crossed and the news of the approach of the English soon was carried to the fort, where its commander, Contrecoeur, was dismayed at the size of the army moving against him. However, a captain in the garrison, Beaujeu, proposed to intercept the English with a party of French and Indians, and at least to harass the advance. Quickly assembling Indians which the French had brought to the vicinity of the fort, after some persuasion he organized an attacking band and inculcated in them a warlike spirit. As soon as the near approach of the English advance was announced the warriors in war paint and fully supplied with ammunition set out in scattered bands to meet the enemy. The English, fording the Monongahela for a second time, advanced into the heavy woods with flanking parties on either side but without scouts in front. As they ascended a gentle slope heavily wooded and with rank undergrowth and grass, they were surprised by a heavy and deadly fire

from the French and Indians led by Beaujeu from a concealed position which enabled them to command the nar-
row road.

BRITISH GRENADIERS AMBUSCADED

The Indians on both flanks taking cover behind rocks and
trees delivered a murderous fire which added to the disorder soon developing. The British Grenadiers returned the
fire once the advance guard had retired to the main body,
which soon was under fire from front to rear. The savages
in their ambuscade enjoyed perfect conditions for their
kind of fighting, and their war-whoops resounded along
the entire front, bringing consternation to the regulars
quite unused to this style of combat. They bravely sought
to establish close order and their officers endeavored to
allay the panic that soon developed. Braddock had five
horses shot under him and ordered his regiments to form
regular platoons, which naturally furnished excellent targets for the concealed Indians whose fire was deadly de-
structive.

Braddock received a mortal wound and was carried from
the field to die. Contrasted with the regulars the Virginia
troops, following frontier practice, took cover wherever
available, and fought to advantage with Colonel Washington acting calmly and seeking to restore order. He had two
horses shut under him and bullets through his clothes, but
suffered no wound. Horatio Gates, commanding companies from New York, and Thomas Gage, also to be known
in connection with the American Revolution, were both
wounded. The Virginians fought with courage and steadi-
ness in striking contrast to the now demoralized English
regulars. Nevertheless the Provincials suffered heavily and
hardly one-fifth of their number escaped alive. In fact,
of the 1200 in the advance party that came under fire
after crossing the Monongahela, over 700 were killed and

From the Painting of C. Schuessele

GENERAL BRADDOCK CARRIED OFF THE BATTLEFIELD OF FORT DU QUESNE

From the Collection of The New York Historical Society

wounded. The slaughter ended in a precipitous rout and a flight across the Monongahela. Fortunately the enemy did not follow, being satisfied with the booty of the battlefield and the wagon trains, along with the collection of scalps.

Rout of the British

The most important outcome of this disgraceful affair was the loss of prestige by the English, not only among the colonists of the frontier who had suffered, but more particularly among the Indians to the West and North. The arrogance of the British officers and their unwillingness to learn the conditions of war as waged by the French and Indians on their western borders were serious factors that had important consequences.

Colonel Dunbar evacuated Fort Cumberland and retired to Philadelphia for winter quarters. The defeat affected colonial relations with the Crown most unfavorably, as a victory for the Royal Arms had been confidently looked for.

From the Painting of F. C. Yohn.   (c) The Glen Falls Insurance Co.

THE BATTLE OF LAKE GEORGE. FIRST ENGLISH SUCCESS AGAINST
THE FRENCH

BATTLE OF LAKE GEORGE

In the scheme of grand strategy of the British ministry the movement planned against Crown Point was hardly successful in its ultimate development, though it was marked by one of the most important engagements in the war, the Battle of Lake George. Here the colonial troops under their own officers and with their own organization, accomplished the memorable defeat of the French and Indians under Baron de Dieskau. To command this colonial expedition Colonel William Johnson, already a notable figure in the Mohawk Valley of New York, was appointed major-general.

Crown Point, situated on the western side of Lake Champlain, first was fortified by the French in 1731, though previously, 1726, they had attempted to establish themselves on the eastern shore of the lake. This action was opposed by Massachusetts, which claimed possession of the ground, a claim that was disputed by New Hampshire and New York. The latter province, then being engaged in a boundary controversy with New Jersey, neglected to move against the French occupation, and a fortified post known as Fort Frederic was built. This was of no small importance as it guarded the north and south route through Lake Champlain in addition to being in dangerous proximity to the English settlements in Vermont and New York.

STRATEGIC CROWN POINT

The location and construction of this post indicated keen foresight on the part of the French, and a corresponding lack of intelligent co-operation by the English colonies. As a result when military operations were planned in 1755, it was realized that this post not only was essential to the French scheme of defense of Canada, but was a perpetual menace to the English colonies, as it afforded an important base for their invasion. Accordingly the decision of England to move against Crown Point was well received in New York and New England, and an army of untrained militia in 1755 was assembled and encamped at the lower end of Lake George.

At Lake George now was to be fought the most important action to take place on the soil of New York State prior to the American Revolution. This battle has been described by many historians, and has been summarized in an interesting paper by the late Morris Patterson Ferris, a member of this Society, published by the Lake George Celebration Committee of the Society of Colonial Wars in the State of New York, in connection with the unveiling of the Lake George Memorial, September 8, 1903. Accordingly significant extracts from this paper are reproduced herewith.

RENDEZVOUS AT ALBANY

"Albany was selected as the rendezvous, and the troops from the different colonies gathered there. Among the officers taking part in the expedition, afterwards distinguished, were Major-General Phineas Lyman, Colonels Ephraim Williams, Timothy Ruggles, Lieutenant-Colonels, Nathan

Whiting, Seth Pomeroy, Captains Philip Schuyler and Israel Putnam.*

"About the first of August, Major-General Lyman led the advance up the [Hudson] river and commenced building a large fort, first named Lyman, afterwards Fort Edward, in honor of Edward, brother of George the Third, and a few days later, General Johnson left Albany with the remainder of the troops, artillery, and stores, accompanied by King Hendrick and his Mohawk warriors. A report reaching the General that the French were concentrated at Fort St. Frederick (Crown Point) with an army of six thousand men, and intended to fortify Ticonderoga (the short carry between Lake Champlain and Lake St. Sacrament), a council of war at once decided that the advance should be made along the road to St. Sacrament. General Johnson reached there with the first fifteen hundred men on the 28th, and immediately went into camp at the head of the Lake, which he rechristened Lake George, in honor of his Majesty and to assert his right of dominion there.

* Major-General Lyman commanding the First Connecticut Regiment was in command of the Connecticut contingent; Colonel Ephraim Williams and Colonel Timothy Ruggles commanded the Third and First Massachusetts regiments, respectively; Lieutenant-Colonel Nathan Whiting was in the Second Connecticut Regiment commanded by Colonel Goodrich; Lieutenant-Colonel Seth Pomeroy was with Colonel Williams' regiment; Captain Philip Schuyler was with the New York troops, and Captain Israel Putnam was with the Connecticut forces. Most of these officers later served in the American Revolution along with others who took part in this expedition.

Indians Refuse to Join French

"On the third of September the Baron de Dieskau, Commander of the French forces in Canada, moved down from Fort St. Frederick to Ticonderoga to begin work on the line of fortifications, which he purposed establishing southward. Information coming of the building of Fort Lyman, he at once embarked with a detachment of two hundred and sixty French Grenadiers, eight hundred Canadians, and seven hundred Indians, sailing down Lake Champlain in canoes to South Bay, thence marching across the country, encamping within a league of Fort Lyman on the evening of the 7th, intending to surprise the Fort the next day. The Indian chiefs were called together to be informed of the plan of attack and to be assigned their positions. They retired for consultation, and soon returned with the statement that the Iroquois (numbering three hundred) would not join in the attack, and as they were the oldest, the rest of the Indians would be obliged to follow their example. They gave as their reason that they had resolved not to act against the English on their own territory; but if the General would lead them against the English camp at Lake St. Sacrament, which was undoubtedly on French soil, they would follow him there.

"Accordingly, yielding to the whim of their Indian allies, always loath to face the cannon of a fort, the French moved on toward the Lake. After marching some hours a prisoner was taken who stated that General Johnson had heard of the contemplated attack on Fort Lyman, and had detached one thousand men who were on their way to reinforce it. Dieskau at once ordered the Canadians to move forward about three hundred paces on the right, and there to lie flat on the ground. He ordered the Indians forward to take a similar position on the left, holding back the French regulars in the centre. No gun was to be fired until the English had reached the end of the cul de sac and then the volley from the French in front was to be supplemented by the fire of the Indians and Canadians on either flank, who were to close up the rear, leaving no escape for the entrapped English.

"General Johnson's forces in the camp on the Lake, consisted of about three thousand provincials and two hundred and fifty Indians. Early in the morning of the eighth of September a Council of war was called, rumors having reached the camp of the proposed attack on Fort Lyman. It was not known exactly where the French were, but it was proposed to send a force of five hundred men to the assistance of the Fort. Hendrick was consulted and replied: 'If they are to fight they are too few, if to be killed they are too many.' The number was doubled. General Johnson then proposed to divide the forces into three parties. Hendrick thereupon picked up several arrows, and handing one of them to General Johnson, asked him to break it. This he did readily. Hendrick then put three arrows together and handed them to General Johnson saying, 'Put them together and you can't break them; take them one by one and you will break them easily.' Hendrick's argument was convincing.*

ATTACK ON FORT LYMAN

"Colonel Ephraim Williams was placed in command of the troops and they set out in two divisions, Colonel Williams leading the first, Lieutenant-Colonel Whiting the second. King Hendrick on horseback at the head of a band of two hundred and fifty Mohawks, preceded the provincials.

---

* The arrows are shown in the Lake George Memorial of the Society of Colonial Wars where are figures of Sir William Johnson and Chief Hendrick.

FORT TICONDEROGA RESTORED

"They proceeded to Rocky Brook, where the French and Indians lay awaiting them. Knowing nothing of the change of plans of the French, whom they supposed near Fort Lyman, they sent out no scouts, but marched directly into the death trap. An accident only saved them. Some of the Senecas, with the French forces, espying their Mohawk brethren fired their muskets into the air as a warning of the ambuscade. Then the war-whoop sounded, followed by the discharge of musketry from behind rocks and trees. Colonel Williams at once spread out the men on the hill to the right, and took his position on the rock on which now rests his monument. He soon fell, and almost at the same time Hendrick's horse was shot from under him, and being unwieldy he could not recover himself, and was stabbed to death with a bayonet.

Lt. Col. Whiting Assumes Command

"Lieutenant-Colonel Whiting succeeded to the command. He saw the danger of his men and immediately ordered a retreat, which he conducted so skillfully that he saved the greater part of his force. The noise of the firing was heard at Lake George, and General Johnson despatching Lieutenant-Colonel Cole with three hundred men to support and protect the retreat, set to work with the utmost vigor with all his remaining forces to construct defences for his camp, preparing a breastwork of felled trees and wagons, and hauling up and placing in position such cannon as he had to cover the river road and approaches.

"It had been Dieskau's purpose to rush forward and enter the camp with the fugitives; but the Iroquois took possession of a rising ground and remained inactive. The other Indians also halted, and a few shots from the cannon soon drove them all to cover in the swamps at either side, and left the French Commander and his veteran regulars unsupported. As the regulars advanced, they halted suddenly about one hundred and fifty yards from the breastworks, trying to call the Indians to their aid. Failing in this, they again advanced, firing by platoons.

"Early in the battle, General Johnson received a wound in the thigh, and retired to his tent, the command then devolving upon General Lyman, who behaved with great bravery.

"The fire from the French made but little impression, while the artillery under the command of Captain Eyre, played upon them with great effect. Dieskau, finding it impossible to break the centre, moved to the right, and attacked the regiments under Colonels Huggies, Williams, and Titcomb. The three regiments resisted the attack resolutely and maintained a hot fire upon the enemy. At four o'clock in the afternoon, about seven hours after the attack in the morning, the Colonial troops, inspired by the thought that victory was theirs jumped over the breastworks with their Indian allies, and charged upon the French, who precipitately retreated, leaving most of their troops dead upon the field. Some prisoners were taken by the Colonials, including Baron Dieskau, who had been wounded. He was taken to General Johnson's tent, where only the General's great influence prevented his being seized by the Indians to expiate with fire the deaths of King Hendrick and the other Mohawk Chiefs.

THE FIGHT AT BLOODY POND

"Colonel Blanchard, at Fort Lyman, having heard the firing, despatched two hundred and fifty men of the New Hampshire and New York regiments, under Captain Maginness, to the assistance of General Johnson. Arriving at the place of the morning conflict, they came upon the enemy's abandoned baggage lying in the road, and advancing, soon caught sight of the Canadians and Indians, about three hundred in number, sitting by Rocky Brook, refreshing themselves from their packs. They fell upon them furiously, and soon few were left to tell the tale. The number of the slain was very great. Their bodies were thrown into the pond, which became so tinged with blood, that it was thereafter known as 'Bloody Pond.'"

After the Battle of Lake George Sir William Johnson did not follow up his success by moving against the French post at Ticonderoga as he might have done, but at the lower end of Lake George built Fort William Henry of wood. Here he left a garrison of six hundred men and dismissed the New England militia to their homes on the approach of winter.

In contrast to the Lake George operation was the expedition to western New York by General William Shirley, appointed in February 1755 a major-general. At Niagara was a wooden fort established by the French in 1726. It was of little strength but its situation was considered of importance, and with Fort Frontenac on the northern shore of Lake Ontario it was the objective of a movement aimed to curb French power in the Northwest. General Shirley's efforts, which involved much road construction, brought him only as far as Oswego on Lake Ontario at the mouth of the river of that name. This was reached on August 21st, with a force of about two thousand men. After building boats, which could not be used on account of storm, and constructing a new fort at Oswego where he placed Colonel

Mercer in command with a garrison of about six hundred troops, Shirley retired from Lake Ontario and returned to Albany and then to Boston. His entire plan failed of accomplishment and the delays were fatal in that they enabled the French to prepare adequately for

offensive movements in this region, and to continue
their plans to consolidate the gains they had made at Fort
Du Quesne.

Objectives for 1756

This lack of success in no way embarrassed General Shirley, who, on the death of Braddock in July, had become
commander-in-chief and received his formal appointment
in August. In December 1755 he held a conference of
colonial governors in New York to plan a series of campaigns for the ensuing year. These objectives included the
capture of Quebec, Frontenac, Toronto, and Niagara, and
then Fort Du Quesne and Detroit.

COLONIAL PROBLEMS

The years 1755-1757 are specially significant not only as showing the British military ineptitude, but also demonstrating a political obtuseness in the attitude towards the colonists, who in their assemblies resisted all infringements of the rights guaranteed under the British Constitution. These they insisted applied to the colonies no less than to the home land. The quartering of troops, taxation without representation, the raising of armies for others to command, all were burdens the Crown now sought to lay on the shoulders of the colonists.

The men of the colonies had enjoyed an unusual degree of liberty and independence for nearly a century and a half. This was due both to their own efforts and to a spirit of freedom associated with the political theories which they sought to achieve, maintain, and develop. In addition there were certain fortuitous circumstances, as where the Mother Country was involved in revolution or foreign wars, and was in no position to enforce abroad its sovereignty and the administrative control appropriate in the case of a Crown colony. A modern historian and student of the American Colonial Period readily could assess a spirit of blame and stubbornness on those who were willing to benefit by their connection with the Kingdom of England, but who were not willing to submit to reasonable regulation and control or obedience to measures required for imperial policy and defense, including the appropriate share of taxation for such objects. But much that was unreasonable and arbitrary now was demanded of the provinces that with little imperial active aid had developed important wealth of resources and growth of population to a point where they were to be reckoned with seriously in any scheme of imperial defense.

The arrogance of men like Braddock, and General James Abercrombie and the Earl of Loudoun shortly to arrive in America by the decision of English Ministers, was only exceeded by their incompetence. Such characteristics soon brought about a condition that did not work for military success and rendered impossible co-operation with the colonists essential to military efficiency and success. Such co-operation was distinctly lacking both on the political as well as the military side, though the colonies voted levies of militia in adequate numbers, which, however, for the most part were untrained and poorly officered. These men the English generals endeavored to adapt to European methods of drill and discipline, completely ignoring their special knowledge of an unsettled country and their training in fighting Indians who now were valued allies of their enemies. Coupled with this was their skill in hunting the wild animals of the forests that roamed fairly close to civilization and their ability to subsist on informal rations.

England Declares War on France

In May 1756 came the formal declaration by England of war on France, a contest that, in addition to its military operations, developed much academic discussion, with claims and counterclaims as to the rights of neutrals and the freedom of the seas. Here in this age-old discussion the claims and assumptions of powers by England were arousing the hostility of the civilized world. But aside from the broader aspect of the struggle, which was of considerable importance, our interest centres in the military activities in North America where England was forced to the conclusion that it must undertake full scale operations and deal with various colonial problems which now must figure in her national policies.

In this struggle there was not only the necessity of defending valuable overseas colonies in America, important both strategically and economically to the Mother Country, but also the realization of a significant evolution of relations between the home government and colonial settlers, who had won for themselves substantial material independence and prosperity as well. This condition was not appreciated by His Majesty's Ministers but it laid the foundation of subsequent events leading to the foundation of the new republic.

Nevertheless Parliament now resolved on active prosecution of the war and the Earl of Loudoun was selected to command in North America. As second in command was appointed General James Abercrombie, who, as stated, had reached Albany on June 25, 1756.

As important campaigns were planned to the North and West against Canada and the French posts to the West, the colonial forces along with the regular troops from England, were assembled at Albany, New York, which, as always, was a gathering point for Provincial troops. Here in 1756 the regiments of New England, with Provincials from New York and New Jersey, amounted to more than 7000 men, and with the British regulars to more than 10,000, in addition to the garrison at Oswego. Accordingly here was a force available for extended campaigns.

The first expedition to be organized by the Earl of Loudoun was designed to capture Louisbourg, which had been restored to the French by the Treaty of Aix-la-Chapelle in 1748. English troops and ships duly were

WOLFE'S INTERVIEW WITH WILLIAM PITT BEFORE HIS DEPARTURE
FOR CANADA

assembled at New York in the spring of 1757, and by June 1st their number was augmented by some six thousand Provincials. The expedition sailed on June 20th for Halifax, where a powerful fleet and some five thousand troops from England were in the harbor ready to set sail for Louisbourg.

CAMPAIGNS AGAINST THE FRENCH

At Halifax Loudoun was informed that a French fleet already was at Louisbourg and that it was of greater strength than his vessels. This anticipation of the English operation was due in large measure to the dilatory actions of Loudoun, and when the French strength was brought to his attention, he felt impelled to abandon the entire enterprise without making any effort either to attack the fortress or meet the French fleet in action.

This was but one of the unfortunate events of the year 1757 that reflected little credit on the British arms and the British commanders.

General Abercrombie, who had been sent over as second in command to Loudoun and was now at Albany, was urged on June 26, 1756, by General William Shirley to add to the garrison at Fort Oswego as the place should be defended at all costs. Accordingly Colonel Bradstreet was ordered to put six months' provisions for 5000 men at that post and corresponding stores. This was done, and on his return Bradstreet reported that a French army was in motion to attack this fort. Such, indeed, was the case, for this important post soon became the leading objective of the French plan of operations. Already, with the arrival of the Marquis de Montcalm, a new era had opened for the French arms. After a study of Fort Carillon at Ticonderoga he quickly assembled a force of Canadians and Indians, which by August 5th he had brought to Sacketts Harbor. On the English side, in addition to the garrison at Fort

Oswego, Colonel Daniel Webb with regular troops was ordered to hold himself in readiness to move to the defense of that post.

Fortifications had been constructed on both sides of the river. Fort Pepperrell or Old Oswego was on the west side at the mouth of the river, while on the opposite bank was Fort Ontario, and in addition various earthworks and an unfinished stockade called New Oswego or Fort George. On August 12, 1756, Montcalm, who had crossed Lake Ontario from Fort Frontenac, began his siege, operating first against Fort Ontario.

Montcalm Captures Fort Oswego

The defenders of the fort were forced to abandon it and take positions across the river at Fort Oswego. Montcalm then occupied a superior height and brought his artillery to bear, killing Colonel Mercer, its commandant, in the course of the bombardment and making a breach in the wall. On August 14th, before the intrenchments could be stormed, the garrison composed of colonial regiments of Shirley and Pepperrell and amounting to some 1600 capitulated and were taken to Quebec as prisoners of war. The forts were completely razed and this important post totally abandoned.

CAPTURE OF FORT WILLIAM HENRY

Again the French assumed the offensive and after the expedition under the Earl of Loudoun had departed for Louisbourg the Marquis de Montcalm determined to collect the Indians and deliver an attack on the English fortifications at Lake George. Accordingly a great gathering of Indians was assembled at Montreal with representatives from some thirty-three tribes, ranging from Acadia to Lake Superior. The co-operation between the French and Indians was complete and the tribes were gathered at Fort St. John on the river Sorel. In a fleet of two hundred canoes they proceeded up the river and across Lake Champlain and landed at Ticonderoga.

Montcalm Surprises the English

Montcalm was here preparing his forward movement, and several minor engagements took place before the main attack was set on foot. For this Montcalm had an army of fifty-five hundred French regulars and Canadians, and sixteen hundred Indians. This force crossed from Ticonderoga to the foot of Lake George where a portion of the army under the Chevalier de Lévis, amounting to some twenty-two soldiers and six hundred Indians, marched along the rough trail on the western side of the lake. The remainder of the Indians in their birch-bark canoes, and

111

WOLFE'S INTERVIEW WITH WILLIAM PITT BEFORE HIS DEPARTURE
FOR CANADA

Montcalm with the rest of the army and the baggage followed in two hundred and fifty boats. A council of war was held and a plan of campaign adopted. On August 2nd the Indians formed a line of canoes across the lake and raised their war cry, taking the English completely by surprise. Those in the outlying camp and barracks withdrew rapidly to the fort, while the soldiers of de Lévis advancing through the woods burned the barracks, drove off cattle and horses, and destroyed the various outposts which they surprised.

Montcalm who had landed about a mile and a half from the fort disposed of his forces in three columns. La Corne with a detachment of Indians and Canadians occupied the road leading to Fort Edward, some fifteen miles away, while de Lévis encamped his force to the south of the fort. Montcalm himself took a position on the west shore of the lake at the edge of the forest. After a day spent in preparations for a siege, Montcalm on August 4, 1757, called on Colonel Monroe commanding the fort to surrender. He stated that he could not answer for the behavior of the Indians in case the fort and its garrison should be captured. Monroe hoping that Colonel Webb, at Fort Edward, with four thousand men, would come to his aid, refused to surrender, and the twenty-two men of the garrison prepared to resist with vigor. The French immediately began a siege, bringing up their artillery from the landing and digging trenches to afford shelter as they advanced.

ENGLISH FORCED TO SURRENDER

Already Israel Putnam with a party of Rangers, who had been on the lake, had discovered the French advance and had urged Webb to oppose the landing. But that officer had withdrawn to Fort Edward where he remained inactive. After the siege was begun Sir William Johnson reached

Fort Edward with Indians and militia, and sought permission to reinforce the fort with a body of volunteers. This was denied by Webb who advised Monroe to surrender.

Monroe failing to receive reinforcement, and with half of his guns out of service and ammunition nearly expended, on August 9th raised a flag of truce. The Indian chiefs participated in the terms of capitulation which permitted the garrison to march out with honors of war and a pledge not to serve against the French for eighteen months. A reciprocal arrangement regarding prisoners was made and the sick and wounded were to receive proper care in the hands of the French. However after the French had taken possession of the fort and the English had marched out and laid down their arms, the Indians fell upon them and robbed and massacred those who were not taken captives. A few of the English escaped to Fort Edward but Fort William Henry was destroyed along with the English vessels and the French secured vast stores of provisions.

Apprehensive of further attacks militia were despatched from Massachusetts and Connecticut to Fort Edward but no advance was made by the French who withdrew to Ticonderoga.

With such serious defeats of the British forces in North America, matters were realized in England to be far from satisfactory and the demonstrated incompetence of the leaders led to a change in the British ministry. William Pitt, who had opposed the foreign policy of the ministry headed by the Duke of Newcastle and conspicuous for mismanagement of affairs, was called upon in November 1756 to take charge of war and foreign affairs. A cabinet with the Duke of Newcastle as nominal prime minister, but with all real power vested in Pitt, was formed. Immediately vigorous measures were undertaken to carry on the war and these at once were reflected in America.

Pitt Enters the Ministry

King George II did not extend to Pitt loyal support and finally dismissed him, but he was forced to recall him and assign to him full control of foreign and military affairs. This was indeed fortunate as Pitt's war policy was marked by unusual vigor and sagacity. There were defeats of French armies in India, Africa, and on the Rhine, with the practical disappearance of the French fleets from the seas. Pitt became virtually an absolute ruler and enjoyed the support of the nation at large by whom he was termed "The Great Commoner."

It was in American relations that his influence is of special concern at the moment, for he reversed former policies of dealing with the colonists and instead of making demands and exactions on them, he announced that English troops would be sent to act with the Provincials in the serious military situation that had developed.

From the Painting of F. C. Yohn.   (c) The Glen Falls Insurance Co.

ABERCROMBIE'S EXPEDITION EMBARKING FOR THE UNSUCCESSFUL ATTACK
ON FORT TICONDEROGA

REPULSE AT TICONDEROGA

In the campaign of 1758 as planned by the British the important feature was to capture the French position at Ticonderoga and then proceed against Montreal. General James Abercrombie determined to lead this expedition in person, and for his second in command had Viscount George Augustus Howe, a grandson of King George I, and a favorite of William Pitt, by whom he was selected for this duty. General Howe was the active spirit of the undertaking, which might have resulted differently were it not for his untimely death.

Abercrombie, as already suggested, failed to establish cordial relations with the Provincials, for whom he had but faintly concealed contempt. He announced that all regular officers would outrank those in the Provincial service of the same grade, and while this point later was yielded, it made for animosities and lack of co-operation. It was agreed that the Provincials under their own officers should advance against the enemy, while the regulars should remain and do duty in the forts. It was said that some of the jealousies and enmities here established were a strong influence in the feeling of the officers of the American army later in the Revolution.

Abercrombie Advances to Lake George

At Ticonderoga Montcalm had strengthened what was a strong defensive work with extra intrenchments built of logs eight to ten feet in height, and in front of them for a hundred yards was an abatis of trees felled with their branches outward.

In the meantime the English and colonial troops had advanced from Albany and were encamped at and below Lake George ready to proceed.

In an interesting paper read before the New York Society of Colonial Wars by a member, William G. Davies, Esq., on November 19, 1900, entitled "Ticonderoga and Crown Point," this operation is graphically described along with a description of the country involved and the principal actors.

Quoting from Mr. Davies' papers, printed in full in the New York Society of Colonial Wars Year Book for 1906-1907, it is possible to present a resume starting with the departure of the English and colonial forces from the southern end of the lake.

British and Provincial Troops Attack

"On the morning of the 5th of July, 1758, the head of Lake George presented a magnificent spectacle. Around the ruins of Fort William Henry were assembled seven thousand British troops of the line, and about ten thousand Provincials, including the best and bravest of both, with the attendant hundreds of non-combatants, forming the finest army up to that time assembled on the Western Continent. For their transportation to Ticonderoga a flotilla was organized, consisting of nine hundred bateaux and one hundred and thirty-five whale-boats, together with a number of rafts to carry the heavy stores, ammunition and artillery. On a beautiful clear day, this imposing pageant swept down the lovely lake, with the sound of

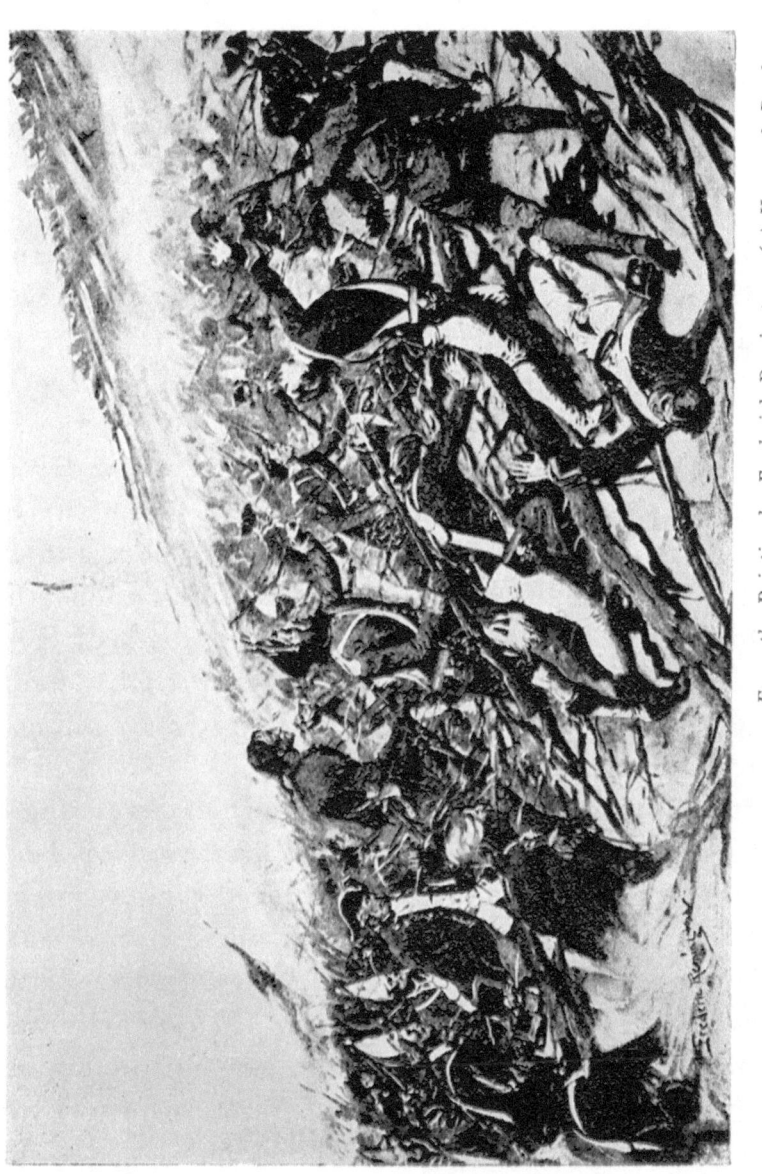

From the Painting by Frederick Remington.   (c) Harper & Brothers

THE STORMING OF FORT TICONDEROGA, 1758

From Vol. 9, "Harper's Encyclopædia of U. S. History"

cheerful voices, the rolling of drums, the exhilarating
blare of trumpets, and the weird screech of the bagpipes
of Lord John Murray's Highlanders. The landing was
effected at noon of the following day in a cove on the west
side of the lake. Here the troops formed in four columns,
and began the advance, without, however, their artillery
and heavy baggage, which had to be left behind until the
bridges, which had been burned by the advance guard of
the enemy, in their retreat, could be rebuilt. Abercrombie's
intention was to hurry forward and carry Ticonderoga
by storm, before the arrival of reinforcements, which were
supposed to be hastening to Montcalm's relief. But the
dense woods and tangled underbrush rendered progress
slow and uncertain, and in the general confusion the advance guard encountered a body of the enemy under De
Trapezèe, who had lost their way. In the skirmish that
followed, Lord Howe fell at the head of his men, and the
utter rout of the French party was but small compensation
for the loss of the brilliant leader . . . The death of Howe
paralyzed the army. With him expired its spirit, its confidence, and hope, all afterwards was prompted by imbecil-
ity, indecision, and folly.

"Abercrombie withdrew his army the next morning to
the landing place, but while he was hesitating, Col. Bradstreet, with Rogers and some four hundred rangers pushed
forward, rebuilt the bridges, and took possession of some
saw mills which the French had erected at the lower rapids
about two miles from Ticonderoga. Thus encouraged
Abercrombie moved his army to the saw mills and sent
forward his engineer Clerk, and John Stark, who was with
the Provincial troops, to examine the enemy's works. The
party returned at dusk, and Clerk reported that the works
would offer only feeble resistance to a charge of the British bayonet, but the more experienced Stark was of a very
different opinion. His advice was rejected by the General

From the Painting by J. P. G. Ferris. (c) *The Glens Falls Insurance Co.*

THE SCOTTISH BLACK WATCH IN THE ATTACK ON FORT TICONDEROGA

as that of an ignorant Provincial, unacquainted with British prowess, and orders were issued, early on the morning of the eighth, to advance without artillery and carry the works at the point of the bayonet.

BRITISH REPULSED AND FORCED TO WITHDRAW

"It is asserted that it was Montcalm's intention to evacuate Ticonderoga without awaiting an attack, as he thought it untenable, and that he did not decide upon a vigorous defense until the morning of the battle. His entire force of fighting men was two thousand nine hundred and ninety-two, and of these four hundred and fifty were irregular troops, who occupied the abatis in front of the works. De Lévis was placed on the right with three regiments—de Boulamarque held the left with an equal force, while Montcalm occupied the centre with the battalions. The declivity towards the outlet was guarded by two companies. Behind each battalion was stationed in reserve a company of grenadiers. Work on the entrenchments was resumed at daybreak, but at the preconcerted signal (an alarm gun), the troops left their labors and assumed their respective stations under arms. Montcalm threw off his coat, and, forbidding his men to fire a musket until he should give the word, calmly awaited the approach of the enemy.

"It was not a battle, but a massacre. Entangled in the trees, confronted by lines of works too high to climb, subjected to a withering and murderous fire from swivels and muskets, the troops held their ground with determined valor. . . . After enduring the enemy's fire without flinching for five hours, the troops retreated in the utmost disorder, having lost in killed and wounded nineteen hundred and sixty-seven men.

"The British had still some twelve thousand men, with plenty of artillery, but their general was thoroughly alarmed, and retreated during the night to the landing, leaving orders for the army to follow him there. On their arrival the next morning, this army of lions led by a stag, was seized with a sudden panic, and would have rushed into the bateaux and sunk many of them had not Col. Bradstreet, by his coolness and presence of mind, prevented such disaster. Abercrombie, it is said, did not breathe freely until Lake George was between himself and the enemy, and his artillery and ammunition fairly on the way to Albany. That pursuit did not follow was due to the feebleness of the enemy, and the impracticability of traversing the forest without Indian guides, which Montcalm did not have. De Lévis went over the track of Abercrombie's army on the morning of the 10th, and found only the vestiges of a routed host."

Abercrombie's sad performance in this campaign led to his replacement by General Jeffery Amherst, who, as is related in the course of a few pages, had captured Louisbourg on July 16, 1758. His promotion took effect in September, but even before that time he had embarked his troops for Boston, and had marched thence through the forest to Lake George which he reached in person in October.

From the Painting by Richard Paton

BURNING OF THE FRENCH MEN-OF-WAR PRUDENT AND BIENFASANT
AT LOUISBOURG

From the Collection of William H. Coverdale

THE SECOND CAPTURE OF LOUISBOURG

The capture of Louisbourg, July 26, 1758, was the first of a series of successes for the English, marking that year as a welcome contrast to the earlier phases of the war. This siege has been well described in a paper entitled "The Second Capture of Louisbourg" read before the New York Society of Colonial Wars by a member, Frederic H. Betts, Esq., at a Court held March 20, 1899.

From this interesting study, printed in the first volume of *Collected Publications of the New York Society of Colonial Wars,* the following account has been abstracted as an interesting summary of the second capture of Louisbourg:

"The expedition was under the command of Admiral, the Hon. Edward Boscawen, as to the Navy, and under General Amherst, as to the Army. Twenty-two ships of the line, fifteen frigates, one hundred and twenty smaller vessels, and a land force variously stated at from nine to eleven thousand men were engaged in the expedition.

"Generals Lawrence and Whitemore and Wolfe were in command of brigades.

"In General Wolfe's brigade served one of the most strenuous opponents, in Parliament, in after years, of the taxation of America, Isaac Barre.

"New York was represented by many, and, among others, by the brave Richard Montgomery, who in after years died for his country, under the walls of Quebec. Richard Monckton, afterwards Governor of the Province of New York, had a prominent place in the expedition.

"Louisbourg was defended by the Chevalier de Drucour and a garrison of from 5000 to 6000 men. He had five ships of the line and seven frigates and smaller vessels, four of which he sunk across the mouth of the harbor to prevent the ingress of the British fleet. . . .

"On June 8, 1758, after waiting some six days for a violent surf to subside, a force, under General Wolfe, consisting of four companies of grenadiers and light infantry, and the New England Rangers, effected a landing. Divisions were rowed to the shore in small boats, under the fire of seven frigates, at three points in Gabarus Bay—White Point, Flat Point, and Fresh Water Cove. Wolfe's division approached Fresh Water Cove, and were met by a hot fire, which caused signals to be given in return, but the boats of Lieutenants Hopkins and Brown, and of Ensign Grant disregarded or misunderstood the orders and pushed on, and Wolfe himself leaping into the surf and wading ashore, came to their support, and the French were driven from their positions.

"On the 11th of June, artillery and supplies were landed, and the French retreated to the fortifications of the town proper.

Louisbourg Besieged

"A few days later, General Wolfe circled the city to the Northern Promontory which projects into the harbor opposite the city, and which was occupied by a lighthouse and fortifications, and succeeded in capturing these points. Placing a battery on Light House Point, on the North of the harbor entrance, he was in a position to command the French battery on the Island in the center of the harbor exit, and to reach the shipping in the harbor itself. . . .

"The siege advanced, step by step, for weeks, drawing the lines tighter and tighter around the doomed city, but marked by little incident except a partially successful sally of the English Earl of Dundonald.

"On July 21st, three of the largest French ships, the *Entreprennant, Capricieux* and *Celebre,* took fire, the *Entreprennant* from shells from the Light House Point or Maine battery, and the others from the *Entreprennant.* On July 22nd, the citadel was burned and the town became practically a ruin. Forty of the fifty-two cannon were disabled. On the 25th of July, two English captains, Laforey and Balfour, entered the harbor at night in small boats and captured and burned the seventy-four-gun ship *Prudent,* and towed out the sixty-four-gun ship *Bienfasant,* with all on board, from under the walls of the town into the Northeastern harbor, where she was secured. . . .

"On the 26th of July, Chevalier Drucour capitulated—yielding to the importunities of the inhabitants, although himself desiring to defend against the impending assault."

This important victory was hailed with great acclaim in England no less than in the American colonies, and services of thanksgiving were held in many New England churches. Pitt's selection of Amherst was more than justified, and from now on the American campaigns enjoyed competent leadership. Amherst in September replaced Abercrombie as commander-in-chief, and from Louisbourg proceeded to Boston, where immediately he began to prepare for an advance to the north and the capture of Ticonderoga.

In the meanwhile during the year 1758 further successes for the British arms were to be scored in the taking of Fort Frontenac and the capture of Fort Du Quesne.

CAPTURE OF FORT FRONTENAC

Later in the year 1758, Col. John Bradstreet, one of the ablest officers of General Abercrombie's army, secured

From the Painting by C. W. Jefferys.   (c) Yale University Press

HAULING THE YANKEE GUNS AT LOUISBOURG

From Vol. 6, "The Pageant of America"

permission to make an attack on Fort Frontenac on the northern shore of Lake Ontario, where Kingston, Canada, now stands. Bradstreet accompanied by forty-two Iroquois Indians embarked in open boats at Oswego and, crossing the lake, landed within a mile of the fort, which was garrisoned by one hundred and ten men under de Noyan. This fort had received no reinforcement, and was in no position to resist the siege which Bradstreet started. A breach in the fortifications was made, and on August 27th the garrison was forced to surrender including not only the fort itself but nine vessels mounting from eight to eighteen guns each. Furs of considerable value and other supplies were gained with the fort. However, on orders from Abercrombie, Bradstreet destroyed not only the fort, but its artillery and stores, and all of the vessels except two which were sent to Oswego with the most valuable part of their cargoes.

A View of LOUISBURG in NORTH AMERICA, taken from the Light House when that City was besieged in 1758.

Printed for Carington Bowles, at his Map & Print Warehouse, N°. 69 in S°. Pauls Church Yard London.

From the Collection of the Society of Colonial Wars

VIEW OF LOUISBOURG IN NORTH AMERICA

THE CAPTURE OF FORT DU QUESNE

The third important event of the year 1758 was the expedition to capture Fort Du Quesne and attempt to remove the stigma of Braddock's defeat. For an interesting description of this expedition it is possible to refer to "An Historical Discourse before The Society of Colonial Wars in the Commonwealth of Pennsylvania" delivered by the Right Reverend Cortlandt Whitehead. S.T.D., Bishop of Pittsburgh, in Christ Church, Philadelphia, November 27, 1898, on the one hundredth and fortieth anniversary of the capture of the fort. On this occasion was unveiled a memorial tablet of Brigadier-General John Forbes, Commander of His Majesty's troops in the Southern Provinces of North America, placed in Christ Church by the Pennsylvania Society of Colonial Wars.

Quoting from Bishop Whitehead's address we learn that—

"The conduct of this expedition was entrusted to General John Forbes. He left Philadelphia about the middle of September, 1758, to join Colonel Bouquet, who was in command of the regulars awaiting his coming since July at Raystown, now Bedford. Bouquet who was a French Swiss, is said to have been the equal of General Forbes in much that constitutes a good commander, a most accomplished and attractive person. To his shrewdness and wariness in dealing with the savages, much of the success of the expedition is to be attributed.

General Forbes Leads the British

"There were many delays in the preparations necessary to be made, principally in obtaining wagons and horses, as Colonel Bouquet's letters show. In August or September, Colonel George Washington, who had been engaged in collecting troops from Virginia, North Carolina and Maryland, proceeded to the rendezvous, followed shortly by General Forbes. Being all assembled, heated dispute arose amongst these leaders with regard to the route to be followed in the campaign against Fort Du Quesne. Colonel Washington, who had traversed the country twice before (1753 and 1754), favored the road which had been used in the ill-starred expedition of General Braddock three years earlier; a road at least familiar and ready for their wagons, but leading through Maryland and Virginia at times, and rather circuitous, as it seemed. Washington's reasons for his opinion are given at length in a letter written at Fort Cumberland, August 2, 1758. General Bouquet, on the contrary, favored a new route laid entirely in Pennsylvania, and had already, on August 23rd, sent Colonel James Burd forward with some troops and wagons, to cut a road through the forest to Loyal Hanna. After much discussion, General Forbes adopted this latter route, although it required the opening of more than one hundred miles of new road through the wilderness between Bedford and Fort Du Quesne. . . .

British Advance with Caution

"The army under General Forbes was composed of twelve hundred Highlanders, three hundred and fifty Regulars, twenty-seven hundred Pennsylvanians, sixteen hundred Virginians, and others from Maryland and North Carolina, and a body of Cherokee Indians; making an army of about six thousand men. Slow and tedious was the journey, described, although without much detail, in letters of the time. On October 14th the main army advanced from Rays-town toward Loyal Hanna, arriving about November 1st. On November 18th further advance was made, covering fifty miles from Loyal Hanna in five days, stopping at New Camp, twenty-two miles west of Loyal Hanna, on November 18th, and arriving on November 24th, much discouraged and fatigued, at a point on Turtle Creek, about twelve miles from Fort Du Quesne. On November 25th, 1758, General Forbes declaring that he would sleep in the fort that night, the army hastily advanced from their encampment, the Provincials in front followed by the Highlanders, and marched with all speed to the point where the junction of the Monongahela and Allegheny had furnished for so long a time an unquestionable vantage in control of the Ohio.

"As the army approached the fort at about six in the evening, they came to a number of stakes on either side of the Indian pathway, on each of which hung the head and kilt of a Highlander, killed or taken prisoner at Major Grant's defeat on September 14th, a few weeks before. We cannot be surprised that this aroused to fury the 'petticoat warriors,' as they were sneeringly dubbed by their antag-onists; and with loud and bitter cries and with swords drawn, they rushed, like mad boars engaged in battle, past the Provincials, who led the column, eager to wreak ven-geance upon the French. Imagine their disappointment, when coming within full view of Fort Du Quesne, they found it desolate, ruined and abandoned—everything burned or blown up, fortifications, ovens, houses, maga-zines, goods of every sort. The French troops had escaped on rafts and boats down the Ohio River. . . .

"There was no blow struck; there were no lives lost in mortal combat; and yet the capture of Fort Du Quesne was a most notable event in the history of our country, worthy of commemoration through all the future years.

"Thus did General Forbes end forever the attempt of the French to press downward from Canada into the Mississippi Valley; and the possession of the great West by the Anglo-Saxon race was forever assured."

As in previous years three grand movements were planned for 1759 with Lord Amherst, who had replaced Abercrombie in the previous September, in supreme command. This plan of campaign included the capture of Ticonderoga and Crown Point by a force under the direct command of Amherst himself, the capture of Quebec by a force under General James Wolfe, and an attempt on Fort Niagara led by General John Prideaux of the English Army with Sir William Johnson as second in command and destined to take over in the course of the siege. From the chief command downward these plans were in striking contrast to those of earlier years, based as they were on a better understanding of conditions both as regards the fields to be fought over and the questions of personnel and administration involved in relations with colonial assemblies and their militia troops.

CAPTURE OF FORT NIAGARA

The first of these military events, chronologically, was the movement against Fort Niagara, to the command of which General John Prideaux was assigned, with Sir William Johnson as second in command. This siege is hardly as familiar as other episodes in the French and Indian wars, but it involved not only a regular siege operation but also a pitched battle. More troops were involved in this movement than fought on the American side either at the not so far distant battle of Lundy's Lane in 1814, or at Bunker Hill in 1775; and the position was an important one strategically. The colonial forces assembled at Oswego, and were transported up the lake in bateaux to a landing in a small bay about four miles east of the fort which was commanded by Captain Pouchot.

SIEGE OPERATIONS BEGUN
A regular siege was begun against the fort, and was carried on with energy and military skill by the attacking force composed of the 44th and 46th regiments, the 4th Battalion of Royal Americans, two battalions of New York troops, and a detachment of the Royal Artillery. They numbered in all about 2200 men, not a few of whom had fought at Fort Ticonderoga in July, 1758. In the course of this operation General Prideaux was killed, July 19, 1759, by

From the Collection of the Society of Colonial Wars

FORT NIAGARA, RESTORED

the explosion of a shell in his own camp, and the command fell to Sir William Johnson by whom the operation was vigorously prosecuted. This force was increased by some 600 Indians on leaving Oswego and later 300 more joined at the siege, making a total of 3100 men.

On July 8th, General Prideaux made a demand for the surrender of the fort which was refused by Captain Pouchot, and two days later parallels were started, the first at a distance of some 700 feet from the fort beginning at about the middle of the front and extending to Lake Ontario. On July 17th a battery was thrown up on the opposite side of the river at Montreal Point and gradually the various parallels were pushed forward. There was active cannonading from both sides and on July 19th General Prideaux was killed passing near a Coehoorn mortar.

A force of French and Indians under D'Aubrey coming to the relief of the fort, advanced by flotilla, and on the morning of July 24th attacked the British behind their breastworks with a force amounting to about 1000 Indians and 600 French. The battle occurred about one and a half miles below Five Mile Meadow at a place called Bloody Run. The French and Indians attacking the English breastworks were met with a delayed but strong fire, three volleys of which brought demoralization and a precipitate retreat in which the defenders, jumping over their breastworks, pursued with fierce zeal. The pursuit continued for some five miles and the attacking force was scattered in every direction. About 120 prisoners were taken including the commanding officer and 16 of his subordinates. At least 150 were killed, which, with wounded and missing, brought the casualties to over 500.

Surrender of the French

A second demand for the surrender of the fort was made after the unsuccessful attempt at its relief, and when the

FRENCH CASTLE, FORT NIAGARA

OFFICERS' ROOM, FORT NIAGARA

French commander, Captain Pouchot, was convinced of the defeat of the forces sent to his aid he capitulated and on July 25, 1759, the French flag was hauled down and this part of New York was forever relieved of French domination. There were 640 prisoners taken and vast quantities of ordnance and supplies. The British loss including the battle of July 24th was 60 killed and 185 wounded.

The capture of Fort Niagara was an important flank movement in the English operations of 1759 and must be considered with the other events of that year.

THE CAPTURE OF TICONDEROGA

In November 1758, General Amherst, who had captured Louisbourg on July 26, and later embarked his troops to Boston, became supreme commander in place of General Abercrombie, as that officer was recalled to England. Already Amherst had marched his army across New England with Lake George as an objective, and now in the spring of 1759 was engaged at Albany.

In an interesting paper on "Ticonderoga and Crown Point" read before the New York Society of Colonial Wars on November 19, 1900, by William G. Davies, Esq., a member, the action at Ticonderoga as developed by General Amherst is interestingly summarized as follows:

"He reached Lake George with an army of about eleven thousand men in June, and late in July it moved down the lake in four columns in a fleet of whale-boats, bateaux, and artillery rafts, and left the boats nearly opposite the former landing place. The army advanced rapidly on the road to the falls, meeting and scattering after a short skirmish a force of French and Indians, and the main body took a position at the saw mills. From prisoners captured it was learned that Montcalm was at Quebec, where that officer met a soldier's death on the 13th of September following, and that Boulamarque commanded at Ticonderoga with thirty-four hundred men. The French withdrew into the fort, and made a show of resistance for several days, while they completed their preparations for evacuating the position. During the night of the 25th of July an explosion took place, and the light of the burning works showed the retreat of the French. Col. Haviland pursued them down the lake with a few troops and took sixteen prisoners, together with some boats laden with powder. Amherst slowly prepared to attack Crown Point, and sent Rogers with his rangers to reconnoitre. But, on the 1st of August, they learned the French had abandoned that fort, and on the 16th, that Boulamarque with his troops was encamped at the Isle of au Noix, at the northern extremity of Lake Champlain, commanding the entrance to the Richelieu. The final conquest of Ticonderoga and Crown Point was achieved with only the loss of Amherst's Adjutant-General, Townsend, a brilliant officer, and about eighty men."

THE CAPTURE OF QUEBEC

The third, and in many respects the most important feature of the year's campaign, as well as the decisive battle of the war, was the siege and capture of Quebec by General James Wolfe. Wolfe was the choice of William Pitt to command the expedition fitting out for this objective, and despite his youth he was made a major-general, to hold that rank in America. The fleet was being prepared in January 1759 and on February 17th of that year General Wolfe sailed on the "Neptune" with Admiral Saunders. There were some twenty-two ships of the line with frigates, sloops of war, and a great number of transports. Louisbourg, their destination, could not be reached on account of the ice, so the fleet went to Halifax. Admiral Holmes's squadron had sailed a few days earlier and had gone to New York, where it was to take on troops destined for the expedition.

BRITISH FLEET ARRIVES

In the meantime the fleet under Admiral Durell had proceeded to the St. Lawrence to intercept the French fleet. By May the vessels of the British fleet, with the exception of Durell's ten ships, were all in the harbor of Louisbourg ready for the expedition. For the land force Wolfe's army amounted to somewhat less than nine thousand men, and he had with him three brigadier-generals, Monckton,

Townshend, and Murray. On June 6th the last ship sailed from Louisbourg and the whole fleet, now reunited, proceeded to the St. Lawrence.

Naturally the British expedition and its general objective was foreseen by the French and the importance of such an attack on Quebec realized. Accordingly the Marquis de Vaudreuil, who in 1755 had succeeded as Governor-General, and the Marquis de Montcalm, in active command of the French land forces, and with a record of successful previous campaigns, were now vitally concerned in developing adequate resistance to any such operation by the British. Every possible measure of defense was undertaken, and ships and troops from France which had eluded the British fleet had come to the reinforcement of Quebec. In addition the Canadians from the surrounding country and many loyal Indians had flocked to the French standards. The disposition of the troops had been planned with great thoroughness, and they had been placed in defenses and at strategical positions along the St. Lawrence River.

In general the French Army was located along the river with its right resting on the River St. Charles, just below the city of Quebec, and the left farther down stream by the Montmorenci, with its gorge and falls, a distance of about eight miles. On the shore were various fortifications; a boom of logs was across the mouth of the St. Charles, while a floating battery, and fireships and rafts were placed along the St. Lawrence River as additional protection. In Quebec the various gates were defended by a garrison of between one and two thousand men. In all, the defenders of the city including Indians and militia amounted to over 16,000 men.

THE FRENCH DEFENSES

The English under the command of General James Wolfe, embarked on their warships and transports, entered the

CAPTURE OF QUEBEC BY ENGLISH UNDER GENERAL WOLFE, SEPT. 13, 1759

From engraving in London Magazine, 1760. Reproduced in Vol. 6, "The Pageant of America"

St. Lawrence and made their way cautiously up the river, the main fleet passing Cape Tourmente so that by June 26, 1759, they were anchored off the south shore of the Island of Orleans. Here the troops were landed and Wolfe sought to develop a plan of campaign against all but insuperable odds and an excellent scheme of defense aided by natural conditions. At first, troops were ferried across the river to Beaumont on the south shore taking up a position at Point Lévis where batteries were erected. Another movement was to the Heights of Montmorenci, where Wolfe intrenched a strong detachment of his force. Later, some of the English ships passed the batteries and anchored above the town.

An attempt at the Heights of Montmorenci was without success due to the precipitous advance of the British Grenadiers, in which the third battalion of Royal Americans participated with heavy casualties.

Above the city of Quebec the French had adequate forces, which had been duly augmented, and they were watching the British squadron that had moved above that city. Strong outposts were planted and both sides were extremely watchful and determined. A series of feints were made by the British commander, who had been quite seriously ill while preparing the attack. On Wednesday, September 12th, Wolfe resolved on the attack. Troops were embarked on the warships and it was proposed to make a landing above the city and scaling the steep wooded banks for an attack on the city itself. The men were placed on boats from the fleet and with a favoring tide passed down the river, where a landing was made. A selected party mounted the heights and overpowered the outpost and guards so that a position was gained, and Wolfe's army was able to form a line of battle on the Plains of Abraham less than a mile from the city. The French were taken completely by surprise, and their forces, dispersed according to their well-conceived plan of defense, were not strong enough at

this point to resist the English. Nevertheless, they speed-
ily assembled their troops and formed for the attack which
was duly delivered and received by the British. The invad-
ers then advanced, halted, and fired. After a few successive
volleys the British charged and in this onslaught Wolfe fell
mortally wounded. Panic seized the French and the city
capitulated on September 18th. General Murray, succeed-
ing to the command when Wolfe fell, was attacked in the
following spring outside the walls of the city in a battle at
Sainte-Foy, that resulted unfavorably to the British.

The French Retire

The French, now commanded by the Chevalier de Lévis,
had sent an urgent request to Versailles for reinforcements
and siege guns and ammunition, and it was an interesting question whether French or English ships would arrive
first. An English squadron eventually arrived and passing
the town overcame the French vessels which contained the
available supplies of food and ammunition. Lévis, accordingly, was forced to raise the siege and retire, which was
done with considerable loss of cannon and other ordnance,
baggage, and supplies.

Although most of the English troops at this battle were
regulars, rangers from the colonies and the third battalion
of Royal Americans participated and the latter suffered
heavy losses in a preliminary encounter near the Montmorenci River.

Aspects of the Seven Years War

The broad aspect of the Seven Years War is shown by the
fact that Provincial troops from the American Colonies
not only served on the North American Continent, but
went to the West Indies. In 1761 an expedition sailed
from Staten Island, New York, against Havana. This force
included British regulars, a Connecticut brigade of 2300

From the Painting by Benjamin West

DEATH OF GENERAL WOLFE ON THE PLAINS OF ABRAHAM

From the Collection of William H. Coverdale

men commanded by General Phineas Lyman, and other
Provincial companies. These troops departed on November 18th, and on the following February 14th received the
surrender of the island of Martinique in addition to taking
other French islands in the West Indies. In July the English forces encamped against Havana, stormed that fortress which on August 13th was captured. The Provincial
forces now experienced an epidemic which proved more
deadly than the battlefield.

The definitive treaty between France and England was
signed at Paris, February 10, 1763, and not only settled
for a while all American questions between these two
nations but brought peace to Continental Europe. France
ceded Canada to England and in fact all her American
territory east of the Mississippi River except New Orleans.
England also received Florida from Spain which country in
turn received Louisiana from France. North America now
was under the control of England though Indian uprisings
figured for a number of years. It should be remembered
that the Seven Years War was practically a world war, but
even at a time of real isolationism the English Colonies
in North America could not think of themselves and their
own interest to the practical exclusion of the European
aspect of the struggle.

In concluding this brief summary of the American Colonial Wars it is desired to emphasize, as far as possible,
conditions influencing the individual colonist and developing the character that found its expression later in the
War for Independence and the founding of the republic.
The Colonial Wars cannot be considered as great military
exploits, where the masses of nations were in conflict, but
rather as uniting small groups influenced by a common
purpose, not merely of self-preservation but in furtherance of ideals brought to the shores of America and there

From the Painting by C. W. Jefferys. (c) Yale University Press
MONTCALM AT QUEBEC
From Vol. 6, "The Pageant of America"

developed into a spirit of independence and liberty. The more the achievements of our colonial ancestors are studied, the more interesting is the realization of their virtues and no less is there recognition of their shortcomings. An appreciation of the true proportions in which their characteristics are found is no less essential than assuming either extreme virtues or moral deficiencies leading to sin and intolerance.

A Civilization Developed

The American colonist for the first time built up a civilization founded on the family and the right of the individual, and to defend this ideal he performed military service with bravery and intelligence. In fact it is quite proper to look for a reciprocal relation between his life as a soldier and as a citizen of a growing community. In this he carried on the Anglo-Saxon tradition, but where such life in the homeland was too often static, in the New World unlimited opportunity made possible a dynamic progress where personal worth and endeavor counted.

While any discussion of colonial civilization and development inevitably tends to the philosophical and economic, yet an attempt has been made to present that special aspect where the individual was only too willing to risk his life in defense of principle, home, and liberty by participating in military measures of offense and defense. He united with his fellow citizens not on the compulsion of a ruler or feudal lord, but by his own free will either as demanded by his duly elected representatives or as a volunteer.

The colonial soldier, accordingly, had first to defend by arms his personal existence and freedom, and then the state which made such opportunity and liberty possible. As a result he had to join with his fellows for organization with discipline of a sort suited for the life he was leading.

As such military service became broader, he had to acquire a proficiency in training, such as participation in European wars might develop. This involved fighting with or against some of the best troops of European armies, but under conditions which to the latter were distinctly novel and where they with profit could learn from the colonial soldier.

EARLY WARS MAKE CIVIC LEADERS

In the colonial service the officers in most cases were leading citizens of the separate plantations and settlements, and in them the rank and file by whom they were elected to such positions had full confidence. Conversely those that served actively against the Indians or the French acquired a strength of authority and resourcefulness that stood them in good stead in their civil relations. What they learned as soldiers in the French and Indian War made them valuable officers in the American Revolution where they served with distinction.

It is not always realized what a large proportion of the population of the American colonists participated actively in the wars just outlined in previous pages, but that the number was large is indeed the case and in the evolution of the United States military defense this has been an item that cannot be neglected by an historian however he may be concerned with economic, political, or theological elements of evolution.

In short, any study of the men of the Colonial Wars should be taken not only with the veneration becoming a descendant but with a critical discrimination and appreciation of the men who laid the foundation of our country.

List of Preferred Reading
THE AMERICAN COLONIAL PERIOD
Compiled by
Society of Colonial Wars in the State of New York

In an endeavor to stimulate reading and study of the American Colonial period, the following list of authoritative works has been compiled by this Society and is here published for the information of the general reader. The list does not pretend to be complete but the books named are historically authentic and are endorsed by the Society.

The Committee that compiled the list is composed of the following members of the Society: Messrs. Louis Effingham de Forest, Noel Bleecker Fox, Earl J. Hadley, Charles W. Lewis, Reginald T. Townsend, and Herbert T. Wade.

GEORGE FREDERICK MILES, *Governor,* 1947

GENERAL WORKS
Adams, James Truslow, *Epic of America* (1931).

—. *Album of American History,* Vol. 1, Colonial Period (1944).

Andrews, Charles McL., *The Colonial Period of American History,* 4 Vols. (1934-1938).

Baldwin, Leland D., *The Story of the Americas,* Chaps. XIII-XVI (1943).

Beard, Charles A., and Bagley, William C., *The History of the American People* (1922).

Beard, Charles A., and Mary R., *A Basic History of the United States.*

Bridenbaugh, Carl, *Cities in the Wilderness.* Period: 1625-1742 (1938).

Channing, Edward, *A History of the United States,* 8 Vols. (1905-1944).

Doyle, John A., *The English Colonies in America,* 5 Vols. (1902-1907).

Encyclopaedia Britannica: See *United States of America, History.* (In last edition, 22: 773-781.)

Gipson, Lawrence H., *The British Empire before the Revolution,* Vols. IV and V, *Zones of International Friction.* Period: 1748-1754 (1939, 1942).

—. Vol. VI, *The Great War for the Empire.* Period: 1754-1757 (1946).

Lodge, Henry Cabot, *Short History of the English Colonies in America* (1881).

Nevins, Allan, and Commager, Henry S., *America: The Story of a Free People,* Chaps. 1-3 (1942).

—. *The Pocket History of the United States* (1943).

Osgood, Herbert L., *The American Colonies in the 17th Century,* 3 Vols. (1907).

—. *The American Colonies in the 18th Century,* 3 Vols. (1924).

Wilson, Woodrow, *A History of the American People,* Vols. I-II (1902).

Winsor, Justin, *Narrative and Critical History of America,* 8 Vols. (1884-1889).

Wright, Louis, *Atlantic Frontier of American Civilization,* Period: 1607-1763 (1947).

PERIOD OF SETTLEMENT AND EARLY INDIAN WARS:

Adams, James Truslow, *The Founding of New England.* Period: to 1690 (1921).

—. *Revolutionary New England.* Period: 1691-1776 (1923).

Andrews, Charles McL., *Narratives of the Insurrections. Period: 1675-1690* (1915).

—. *The Fathers of New England* (1919).

Baird, Charles W., *History of the Huguenot Emigration to America,* 2 Vols. (1885).

Beer, George Louis, *The Origin of the British Colonial System* (1908).

—. *The Old Colonial System,* 1660-1754, 2 Vols. (1912).

Benedict, Robert D., *The Pequot War.* Period 1637. (In N. Y. Society of Colonial Wars Year Book for 1906-1907).

Bodge, George M., *Soldiers in King Philip's War.* Period: 1675-1676 (Second Edition 1906).

Bolton, Charles K., *The Real Founders of New England* (1929).

Bolton, Herbert E., and Marshall, Thomas M., *The Colonization of North America,* 1492-1783 (1920).

Bourne, Edward G., *Spain in America,* 1450-1580 (1904).

Church, Thomas, *The History of Philip's War also of the French and Indian Wars at the Eastward.* 1689, 1690, 1692, 1696, 1704. (First published in 1716. See H. M. Dexter's Edition of 1865.)

Coleman, Roy V., *The First Frontier.* Period: Early Seventeenth Century (1948).

De Forest, Louis Effingham and Anne L., *Captain John Underhill.* Period: Military Service 1631-1665 (1934).

Drake, Samuel A., *The Border Wars of New England.* Period: King William's War, 1689-1697, and Queen Anne's War, 1701-1714 (1897).

Ellis, George W., and Morris, John E., *King Philip's War.* Period: 1675-1676 (1906).

Fiske, John, *The Discovery of America,* 2 Vols. (1892).

—. *The Beginnings of New England.* Period: to 1689 (1889).

—. *The Dutch and Quaker Colonies in America,* 2 Vols. (1899).

—. *New France and New England*. Period: to 1759 (1902).

Griffis, William E., *The Story of the Walloons* (1923).

Hubbard, William, *History of the Indian Wars in New England*. Period: to 1676. (First published 1677. See S. G. Drake's Edition of 1865.)

Lincoln. Charles H., *Narratives of the Indian Wars*. Period: 1675-1699 (1913).

Lorant, Stefan. *The New World. The first pictures of America*. Period: 1562-1565, 1585-1590 (1946).

Morison, Samuel Eliot, *Builders of the Bay Colony* (1930).

—. *Admiral of the Ocean Sea*, 2 Vols. Period: Columbus (1942).

Parkman, Francis. *Pioneers of France in the New World*. Period: Ribault in Florida and South Carolina 1558-1568, and Champlain's Career 1604-1635 (1885).

Penhallow, Samuel, *The History of the Wars of New England with the Eastern Indians*. (First published 1726. See Edition of 1859.)

Sylvester, Herbert M., *Indian Wars of New England*, 3 Vols. (1910).

Thwaites, Reuben Gold. *The Colonies*, 1492-1750 (1923).

Tyler, Lyon G., *England in America*, 1580-1652 (1904).

Wertenbaker. Thomas J., *The Puritan Oligarchy; the Founding of American Civilization* (1947).

LOCAL HISTORIES AND SPECIAL ITEMS

Andrews, Matthew Page, *History of Maryland: Province and State* (1929).

Brodhead, J. R., *History of the State of New York*, 2 Vols. (1871, 1874).

Connor, R. D. W., *North Carolina: Rebuilding an Ancient Commonwealth*, 1584-1925, 4 Vols. (1928-1929).

Conrad, Henry C., *History of the State of Delaware*, 3 Vols. (1908).

Dunaway, Wayland F., *History of Pennsylvania* (1935).

Farrand, Max, *The Fathers of the Constitution* (1921).

Fisher, Sidney G., *The Quaker Colonies* (1919).

Fornance, Joseph K., *The Pennymite Wars*. Period: 1769-1775. (Society of Colonial Wars in Pennsylvania, 1941.)

Hart, Albert B., *National Ideals Historically Traced,* 1607-1907 (1907).

Johnson, Amandus, *Swedish Settlements on the Delaware,* 1638-1664, 2 Vols. (1911).

Johnston, Mary, *Pioneers of the Old South* (1918).

Jones, Charles C., Jr., *The History of Georgia,* 2 Vols. (1883).

Lee, Francis B., *New Jersey as a Colony and as a State,* 4 Vols. (1902).

McCrady, Edward, *The History of South Carolina under the Proprietary Government,* 1670-1719 (1897).

—. *The History of South Carolina under the Royal Government,* 1719-1776 (1901).

Morison, Samuel Eliot, *Maritime History of Massachusetts* (1902).

Nettels, Curtis P., *The Roots of American Civilization* (1938).

Scharf, J. Thomas, *History of Maryland,* 3 Vols. (1879).

—. *History of Delaware,* 2 Vols. (1888).

Van Doren, Carl, *Benjamin Franklin* (1938).

Van Rensselaer, Mrs. Schuyler, *History of the City of New York in the Seventeenth Century,* 2 Vols. (1909).

Wertenbaker, Thomas J., *Torchbearer of the Revolution*. Period: Bacon's Rebellion in Virginia, 1676 (1940).

THE LATER FRENCH AND INDIAN WARS:

Beer, George Louis, *British Colonial Policy,* 1754-1765 (1907).

De Forest, L. Effingham, Editor, *The Journals and Papers of Seth Pomeroy*. Period: Louisbourg Expedition, 1745, and Crown Point, 1755. (Society of Colonial Wars in New York, 1926.)

—. *Louisbourg Journals*. Period: 1745. (Society of Colonial Wars in New York, 1932.)

Drake, Samuel G., *A Particular History of the Five Years French and Indian War in New England and Parts Adjacent. 1744-1749* (1870).

Emerson, George D., *The Niagara Campaign of 1759* (1909).

Gabriel, Ralph H., *Lure of the Frontier*. Period: Dunmore's War, 1774 (one chapter) (1929).

Greene, Evarts B., *Provincial America*. Period: King William's War, 1689-1697, and Queen Anne's War, 1701-1714 (1905).

Halsey, F. W., *The Old New York Frontier* (1901).

McLennan, J. S., *Louisbourg from its Foundation to its Fall* (1918).

Pargellis, Stanley McC., *Lord Loudon in North America*. Period: 1755-1763 (1933).

Parkman, Francis, *History of the Conspiracy of Pontiac*. Period: Western Frontier 1763-1764 (1851).

—. *Historical Account of Bouquet's Expedition against the Ohio Indians*. (Originally published 1765. Parkman's Edition, 1868.)

—. *A Half Century of Conflict*. Period: Queen Anne's War, 1701-1714, and King George's War, 1744-1748 (1892).

—. *Montcalm and Wolfe*. Period: 1756-1759 (1884).

Sargent, Winthrop, *History of an Expedition against Fort Du Quesne*. Period: Braddock's Expedition, 1755 (1856).

Shippen, Edward, *Memoir of Henry Boquet, Brigadier General, 1719-1765*. (Society of Colonial Wars in Pennsylvania, 1900.)

Thwaites, Reuben Gold, *France in America*. Period: Entire military history (1905).

Wrong, George M., *The Conquest of New France* (1918).

ORIGINAL NARRATIVES

Amherst, Jeffery, *Journal,* Edited by J. Clarence Webster. Period: 1758-1763 (1931).

Bradford, William, *Of Plimoth Plantation.* (First published 1856) (1912).

Claus, Daniel, *Narrative of his Relations with Sir William Johnson and Experiences in the Lake George Fight.* Period: 1755. (Society of Colonial Wars in New York, 1904.)

Commager, Henry S., Editor, *Documents of American History,* Vol. I (1935).

Commager, Henry S., and Nevins, Allan, *The Heritage of America* (1939).

Gardiner, Lion, *Relation of the Pequot Warres.* (Acorn Club Edition, 1901; also Mass. Hist. Collections, 3 ser., III: 131; X: 185.)

Mackellar, Patrick, *Journal of the Siege of the Havana by an Officer and a Correct Journal of the Siege by P.M., Chief Engineer.* Period: 1762. (Both originally published 1762. See Edward Everett Hale's edition, 1898.)

Nicholson, Francis, *Journal of Col. Nicholson at the Capture of Annapolis* (Port Royal, Nova Scotia). Period: 1710. (Collections Nova Scotia Historical Society, 1878.)

Pepperrell, William, *Journal of Sir William Pepperrell.* Period: Expedition to Louisbourg, 1745 (1910).

Putnam, Rufus, *Journal of General Rufus Putnam in the French and Indian War,* 1757-1760 (1886).

Rogers, Robert, *Journals of Major Robert Rogers,* 1755-1760 (1883).

—. *Diary of the Siege of Detroit in the War with Pontiac,* Edited by F. B. Hough (1860).

Smith, John, *The Generall Historie of Virginia, New England and the Summer Isles.* (First published 1624. See Glasgow Edition, 2 Vols. 1907.)

Underhill, John, *Newes from America*. Period: Pequot War, 1637. (First published, London, 1638. See reprint, 1902.)

Washington, George, *Journal of Col. George Washington*. Period: 1754 (1893).

See also the following, elsewhere cited: *Journals and Papers of Seth Pomeroy, Louisbourg Journals, Narratives of the Insurrections,* and *Narratives of the Indian Wars.*

FICTION

Chambers, Robert W., *Cardigan*. Period: Mohawk Valley, N. Y., 1774-1775 (1901).

Cooper, James Fennimore, *The Deerslayer*. Period: New York Frontier, 1740-1745.

—. *The Last of the Mohicans*. Period: New York Frontier, Siege of Fort William Henry, 1757.

Forbes, Esther, *Paradise*. Period: Massachusetts Bay Colony, 1640.

Roberts, Kenneth, *Northwest Passage*. Period: Northwestern Frontier and Expedition against Canada, 1759-1766 (1937).

SOCIAL BACKGROUND

Adams, James Truslow, *Provincial Society*. Period: 1690-1763 (1927).

Andrews, Charles McL., *Colonial Self-Government*. Period: 1652-1689 (1904).

—. *Colonial Folkways* (1919).

Beard, Charles A., and Mary R., *The Rise of American Civilization,* Chaps. I-IV (1933).

Bruce, Philip A., *Social Life in Virginia in the 17th Century* (1907).

Calhoun, Arthur W., *A Social History of the American Family,* Vol. 1 (1917).

Dow, George Francis, *Domestic Life in New England in the 17th Century* (1925).

Earle, Alice Morse, *Home Life in Colonial Days* (1898).

Fisher, Sidney G., *Men, Women, and Manners in Colonial Times,* 2 Vols. (1898).

Forbes, Esther, *Paul Revere and the World He Lived In* (1942).

Fox, Dixon Ryan, *Caleb Heathcote.* Period: New York Province, 1692-1721 (1926).

—. *Yankees and Yorkers* (1940).

Goodwin, Maud W., *Dutch and English on the Hudson* (1919).

Halsey, R. T. H., and Tower, Elizabeth, *The Homes of our Ancestors* (1937).

O'Conor, Norreys J., *A Servant of the Crown* (John Appy, Judge Advocate). Period: 1756-1761. (Society of Colonial Wars in New York, 1938.)

Parrington, Vernon L., *The Colonial Mind* (1927).

Singleton, Esther, *Social New York under the Georges,* 1714-1776 (1902).

Schlesinger, Arthur M., *The Colonial Merchants and the American Revolution,* 1763-1776 (1918).

Weeden, William B., *Economic and Social History of New England,* 1620-1789, 2 Vols. (1890).

Wertenbaker, Thomas J., *The First Americans,* 1607-1690 (1927).

—. *Planters of Colonial Virginia* (1922).

—. *The Founding of American Civilization* (1938).

—. *Virginia under the Stuarts* (1914).

—. *The Old South* (1942).

Williston, George F., *Saints and Strangers* (The Mayflower Company) (1945).

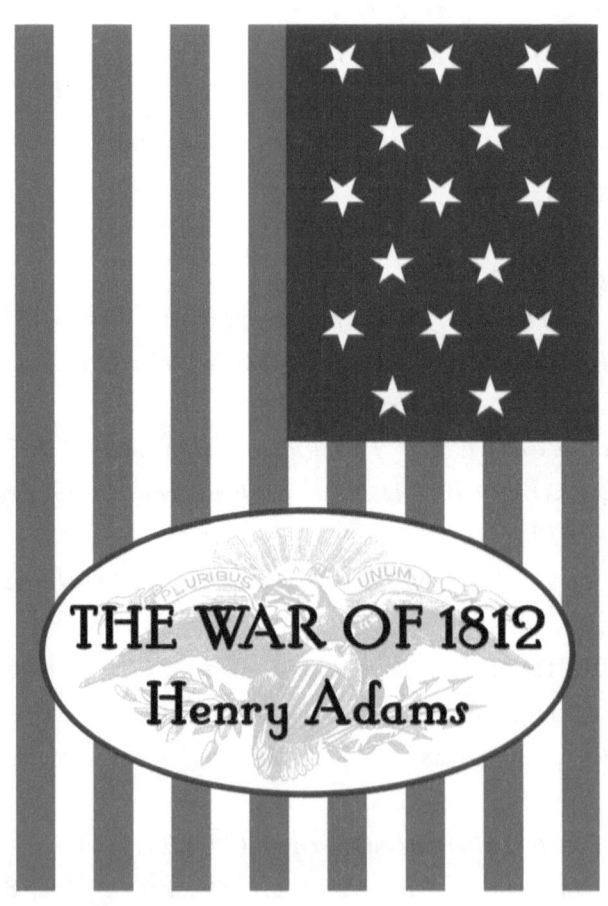

THE WAR OF 1812
Henry Adams

YORKTOWN

THE STRATEGY, PEOPLE, AND EVENTS
SURROUNDING THE FINAL BATTLE IN THE
AMERICAN WAR OF INDEPENDENCE

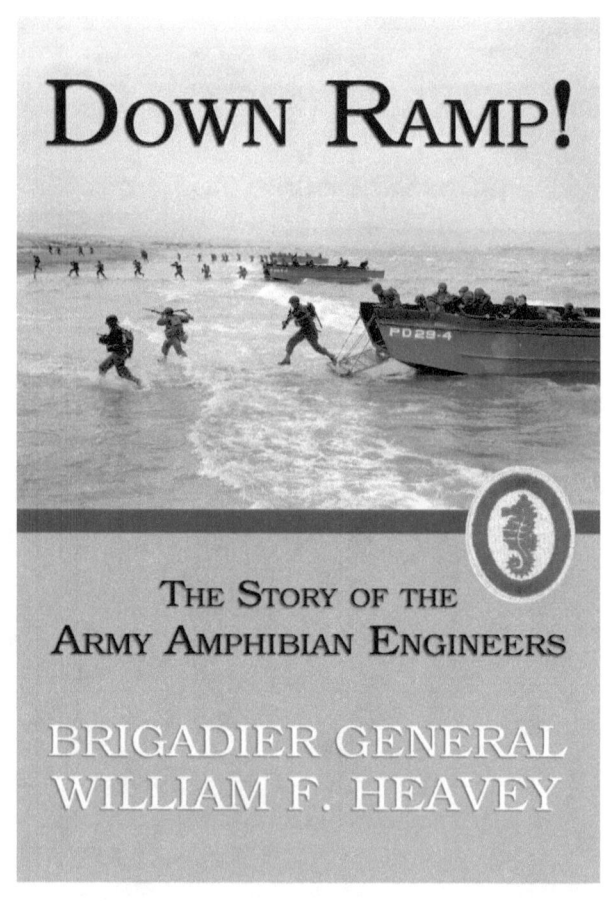

HANDBOOK
FOR SPIES

ALEXANDER FOOTE

COACHWHIP PUBLICATIONS
ALSO AVAILABLE

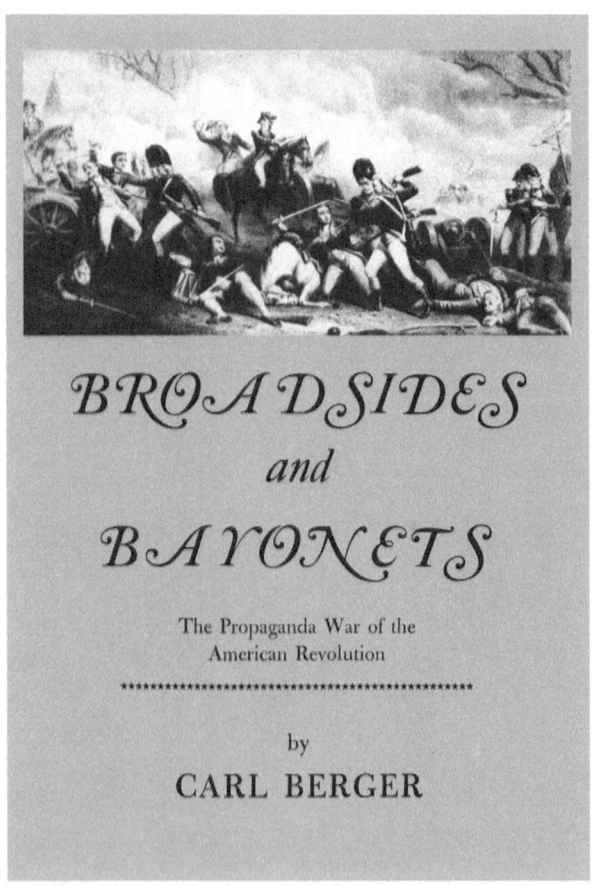

BROADSIDES
and
BAYONETS

The Propaganda War of the
American Revolution

****

by
CARL BERGER

BASTOGNE

The Story of the First Eight Days
In Which the 101st Airborne Division Was
Closed Within the Ring of German Forces

COLONEL S. L. A. MARSHALL

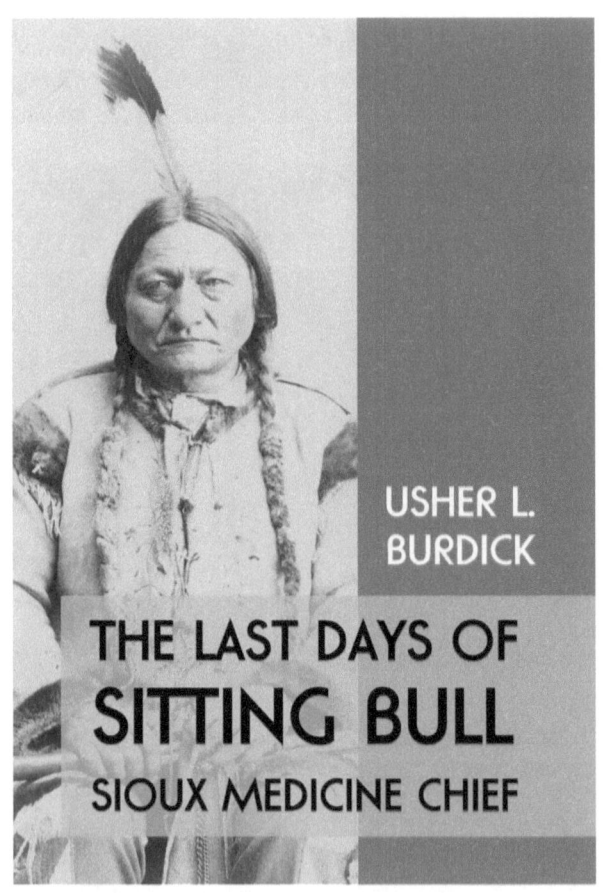

USHER L.
BURDICK

THE LAST DAYS OF
SITTING BULL
SIOUX MEDICINE CHIEF

COACHWHIPBOOKS.COM (PRINT)
COACHWHIP.COM (EPUB)

PIRATE AND
BUCCANEER DOCTORS
Leo Eloesser